Twelfth Night

ARDEN STUDENT SKILLS: LANGUAGE AND WRITING

Series Editor:

Dympna Callaghan, Syracuse University

Published Titles

The Tempest, Brinda Charry
Macbeth, Emma Smith
Romeo and Juliet, Catherine Belsey

Forthcoming Titles

Hamlet, Dympna Callaghan
Othello, Laurie Maguire
King Lear, Jean Howard
A Midsummer Night's Dream, Heidi Brayman Hackel

Twelfth Night

Language and Writing

FRANCES E. DOLAN

B L O O M S B U R Y
LONDON • NEW DELHI • NEW YORK • SYDNEY

Bloomsbury Arden Shakespeare

An imprint of Bloomsbury Publishing Plc

50 Bedford Square
London
WC1B 3DP
UK

1385 Broadway
New York
NY 10018
USA

www.bloomsbury.com

Bloomsbury is a registered trade mark of Bloomsbury Publishing Plc

British Library Cataloguing-in-Publication Data
A catalogue record for this book is available from the British Library.

ISBN: HB: 978-1-4725-1834-7
PB: 978-1-4081-7174-5
ePDF: 978-1-4725-1832-3
ePub: 978-1-4725-1831-6

Library of Congress Cataloging-in-Publication Data
A catalog record for this book is available from the Library of Congress.

Typeset by Fakenham Prepress Solutions, Fakenham, Norfolk NR21 8NN
Printed and bound in Great Britain

CONTENTS

SERIES EDITOR'S PREFACE

This series puts the pedagogical expertise of distinguished literary critics at the disposal of students embarking upon Shakespeare Studies at university. While they demonstrate a variety of approaches to the plays, all the contributors to the series share a deep commitment to teaching and a wealth of knowledge about the culture and history of Shakespeare's England. The approach of each of the volumes is direct yet intellectually sophisticated and tackles the challenges Shakespeare presents. These volumes do not provide a shortcut to Shakespeare's works but instead offer a careful explication of them directed towards students' own processing and interpretation of the plays and poems.

Students' needs in relation to Shakespeare revolve overwhelmingly around language, and Shakespeare's language is what most distinguishes him from his rivals and collaborators – as well as what most embeds him in his own historical moment. The *Language and Writing* series understands language as the very heart of Shakespeare's literary achievement rather than as an obstacle to be circumvented. This series addresses the difficulties often encountered in reading Shakespeare alongside the necessity of writing papers for university examinations and course assessment. The primary objective here is to foster rigorous critical engagement with the texts by helping students develop their own critical writing skills. *Language and Writing* titles demonstrate how to develop students' own capacity to articulate and enlarge upon their experience of encountering the text, far beyond summarizing, paraphrasing or 'translating' Shakespeare's language into a more palatable, contemporary form. Each of the volumes in the series introduces the text as an act of specifically literary language and shows that the multifarious issues of life and history that Shakespeare's work addresses cannot be separated from their expression in language. In addition, each book takes students through a series of guidelines about how to develop viable undergraduate critical essays on the text in question, not by delivering interpretations, but rather by taking readers step-by-step through the process of discovering and developing their own critical ideas.

All the books include chapters examining the text from the point of view of its composition, that is, from the perspective of Shakespeare's own process of composition as a reader, thinker and writer. The opening chapters consider when and how the play was written, addressing, for example, the extant literary and cultural acts of language, from which Shakespeare constructed his work – including his sources – as well as the generic, literary and theatrical conventions at his disposal. Subsequent sections demonstrate how to engage in detailed examination and analysis of the text and focus on the literary, technical and historical intricacies of Shakespeare's verse and prose. Each volume also includes some discussion of performance. Other chapters cover textual issues as well as the interpretation of the extant texts for any given play on stage and screen, treating for example, the use of stage directions or parts of the play that are typically cut in performance. Authors also address issues of stage/film history as they relate to the cultural evolution of Shakespeare's words. In addition, these chapters deal with the critical reception of the work, particularly the newer theoretical and historicist approaches that have revolutionized our understanding of Shakespeare's language over the past 40 years. Crucially, every chapter contains a section on 'Writing matters', which links the analysis of Shakespeare's language with students' own critical writing.

The series empowers students to read and write about Shakespeare with scholarly confidence and hopes to inspire their enthusiasm for doing so. The authors in this series have been selected because they combine scholarly distinction with outstanding teaching skills. Each book exposes the reader to an eminent scholar's teaching in action and expresses a vocational commitment to making Shakespeare accessible to a new generation of student readers.

Professor Dympna Callaghan
Series Editor
Arden Student Skills: Language and Writing

PREFACE

Beguile the time and feed your knowledge

Twelfth Night has garnered a great deal of critical attention in the last few decades, especially from critics interested in gender and sexuality. It also remains popular with theatre audiences in part because its attention to the complexities of romantic relationships still feels current. *Twelfth Night* is a particularly good choice for this series not only because it is popular but because the concerns that make it so can best be approached through slow and careful reading. If you do not attend to the specifics of the play's language, you cannot get at the play's pleasures or grapple with its challenges. For example, simply by tracking the pronouns and tenses in Viola's 'Patience on a monument' speech (2.4), you can begin to open up the complexities of gender identity and sexual desire, and the slippery nature of time, in the play.

We cannot even understand the play's plot without reading carefully. At the end of the play, when identities are revealed and matches made, Olivia sends for Malvolio. But why? As Ann Jones and Peter Stallybrass point out, Olivia sends for him 'For the simple reason that he is responsible for the imprisonment of the Captain with whom the play began. And the Captain has Viola's clothes, the clothes that Orsino calls for so that Cesario can be transformed back into Viola' (199). Whereas the play concludes with the *failure* of Cesario to become Viola, then, many productions ignore this to put

Viola back in her 'maiden's weeds' (or women's clothing). A student will miss the complexity of the play's conclusion – and the striking stage picture of Orsino and Cesario coupled – if he or she reads too quickly, relies on film versions or depends on plot summary from online study guides, which tend to get this wrong. The Sparknotes plot summary, for instance, explains only that 'someone remembers Malvolio' and makes no mention of Viola's clothes. The more detailed plot summary on that site says that Viola casts off her masculine disguise: 'First she casts it off through speech, as she lets everyone know that she is really a woman, and then through deed, as she talks about putting back on her women's clothing, or "maiden weeds".' Even though the summary goes into some of the ambiguities of gender and sexual identity, it confuses words and deeds, since talking counts as doing, and it does not nail down the specifics of where Viola's clothes are and how that shapes the plot. In short, despite all of the study aids available, a baffled student has no recourse but to return to the play itself. This volume seeks to arm that baffled student with the tools to find his or her own answers.

While the book itself hopes to be a companion and tour guide, I also advise readers throughout to turn to the play itself for clues to its meaning. *Twelfth Night* is a play filled with quests and questions, with characters looking for love and for answers. As readers and viewers, we join them in that process of inquiry. Some of our questions are answered and searches resolved by the end of the play. But not all of them. More important than resolving our questions is the way that the play models for us a process of questioning and seeking.

This is why I am most interested in helping you to recognize and explore the play's complexities rather than trying to explain or simplify them. When we think about the play providing us with clues or prompting our research, we might at first think about this in terms of allusions – those moments when the play refers or gestures outside itself and we must draw on our knowledge or on research to understand the reference. For example, Shakespeare often alludes to classical myths and to the Bible. These allusions may or may not be familiar to readers at first glance. But we can usually track them down with a little effort. Sometimes the plays make references to contemporary fashions or scandals or politics. These, too, can often be tracked down.

However, allusions sometimes prove elusive. For example, a topical reference to what was in the news when the play was first performed can sometimes become obscure. For example, when Sir Toby asks Sir Andrew about why he hides his dancing skills he does so in this way: 'Are they like to take dust, like Mistress Mall's picture?' (1.3.121–2). This may refer to some forgotten joke or reference. Some critics think that Mistress Mall may be the Virgin Mary and the reference to her hidden picture a reference to the decline in attention to Mary after the Reformation, a dramatic set of reforms of religious practise that, among other things, downplayed devotion to Mary. Others don't see the reference to the Virgin Mary here and suggest this refers instead to some more mundane Mistress Mall who was in the news or a subject of gossip or jest in the early seventeenth century. In drawing your attention to the mysterious Mistress Mall, my point is to advise you from the start that not all mysteries can be solved and not all inquiries are a simple matter of looking at the notes or searching outside the play for explanations of what seem bewildering inside it. Instead, the play sometimes works to unsettle our certainties. That is when its invitations to us to question and examine are the most profitable, in my view.

Let's establish from the start that *Twelfth Night* is a play and not a novel. Although many people mistakenly refer to all literary works as 'novels', the term novel describes a lengthy prose fiction. This form of literature did not come into its own until the eighteenth century, although some of Shakespeare's contemporaries wrote prose fictions, such as romances, that prepared the way for the novel. Shakespeare himself did not write prose fictions. He wrote plays (or dramas) and poems. Shakespeare wrote different kinds of plays: histories, tragedies and comedies such as *Twelfth Night*. Late in his career, he wrote plays that combine these genres in ways that defy easy categorization. These plays, which include *The Tempest*, are sometimes called simply 'late plays'. As we will see, all of Shakespeare's plays include a great deal of poetry. Since plays are scripts for performance, they record dialogue among characters. They do not provide a narrator who would govern our experience of the story, as novels and short stories do. Instead, we must observe the interplay among characters for ourselves. While some characters have more lines than others, and some have long speeches in which they give us particular insight into what they think and feel, no one character controls our access to information or perspective on events. A page of a play is a series of characters' names – called speech prefixes – followed by the lines each character says. In Shakespeare's plays, stage directions tend to be minimal. When we read a play, then, we have to be able to imagine people speaking the lines. No narrator tells us what a character looks like, or how she says the lines, or what the room looks like in which he stands. Our imaginations have to do a lot of the work.

If you just read straight down the page, without paying much attention to the shift from one speaker to another, you will soon be lost. You have to be willing to visualize the characters and the action. Many students turn to film to help prime the pump of visualization. This is an excellent strategy. However, one of my students once said that she felt that films 'incarcerated' her imagination because once she saw a film version, she had a hard time picturing the characters or the world differently. So keep in mind that what can be daunting about reading plays is also empowering. You can cast and costume the play, design the sets and direct line readings and movement or blocking. When you have the opportunity to see a play in performance you will be able to combine some of the freedoms of imagining it with the inspiration of seeing characters assume flesh and interact with one another. In a film, the camera directs where we look. When we see a play onstage, the director and lighting designer might try to guide what we notice or focus on. But, ultimately, the choice is ours. For you, a minor character might steal the show.

At one point in the play, Antonio encourages his friend Sebastian to 'beguile the time and feed your knowledge / With viewing of the town' (3.3.41–2). Here, I hope you will beguile the time and feed your knowledge with reading of this book. Students in literature classes sometimes question what they're learning and what they're being tested on. Are they learning anything transferable to another class or activity? What's the 'take away', as an American journalist might ask? The take away for this volume is a vocabulary for literary analysis, a set of reading skills that one might use not only to understand this play more deeply but to get more out of any text, and some concrete strategies for transforming close reading into original interpretation and clear, compelling writing. Above all, I hope you will learn to develop and trust your observations. If you are confused or resistant, that's something to pursue rather than pass over. A question or a befuddlement is often the start of an eye-opening interpretation. As I hope you'll see in this book, the most interesting and influential critical readings of *Twelfth Night* have emerged out of critics' close attention to detail and the kinds of questions you will raise yourself. So start by trusting your questions. Professors soon learn that whenever a student says 'this might sound stupid but ...' what follows is often a great question, an acute observation or a fresh and surprising insight. When students fear they are stating the obvious or asking a dumb question they are often on the brink of deeper understanding. Critics don't necessarily have less obvious observations or smarter questions. Instead, they have the confidence to press on with what they notice and follow where it leads them.

Here is a quick overview of the chapters to come. The Introduction surveys different points of entry into the play and explores some of the ways in which the play is located in history. In Chapter 1, 'Language in print: 'tis poetical', we cover the basics of grammar, figures of speech, and reference tools. When Cesario first meets Olivia, she tells him that he need not replay the praise Orsino has instructed him to deliver. But Cesario says 'Alas, I took great pains to study it, and 'tis poetical' (1.5.189–90). In this chapter, we focus on what makes Shakespeare's language 'poetical' and attempt to allay many students' fear of poetry. Chapter 2, 'Language, character and plot', focuses on how language is not just the clothing on the skeleton of the play but inseparable from both character and plot. Through a series of examples, we will discuss how to attach speeches to characters, the plot and central themes and patterns of meaning, and how to think about the intimate interrelationship between plot and imagery in this play. At the end of the chapter, exercises in pairing the play with other texts and in dividing it into parts or roles will offer strategies for sharpening your understanding of how language, plot and character work together. Chapter 3, 'Language through time', focuses on words and expressions in the play that have changed over time and so might be inaccessible to you at first but that offer insight into the play and into the time when and place where it was first performed. At the end of this chapter, we focus on doing the spade work of textual analysis that will enable you to gather evidence in support of an argument. You'll find a checklist to use as a first step in analysing a passage as well as exercises on editing a passage or creating your own 'commonplace book'. In this chapter and the preceding one, I encourage you to experiment with forms of writing that were specific to the sixteenth and seventeenth centuries and might open up new ways of thinking about the play and paying closer attention to its language – the part scroll and the commonplace book. The final chapter, 'From reading to writing', poses questions worth thinking and writing about and some strategies for making the leap from evidence collection and analysis to argument as well as pointers for building the components of a paper, including introductions, paragraphs and conclusions.

Introduction – ways in

The very title of Shakespeare's *Twelfth Night* alerts us to the fact that most readers and viewers need glosses or notes to understand Shakespeare, however often we are told that the plays are 'universal' in their appeal and relevance. What does 'Twelfth Night' mean? The subtitle 'or what you will' doesn't clarify much. It sounds like a version of the dismissive 'whatever'. Twelfth Night is a Christian holiday, 6 January, which brings the winter holiday season – especially the 12 days of Christmas celebrated in a familiar carol – to a close. The play might first have been performed on this holiday. But the first recorded performance is a month later on 2 February 1602. Twelfth Night was traditionally celebrated through what was called inversion or misrule, in which participants temporarily exchanged social positions so that the high became low and vice versa and the normal order of things was turned upside down. While the title of the play might simply refer to its first performance, it might also refer to the disguise, mistaken identities, wordplay and confusion at its centre. The title certainly starts many modern readers off at a disadvantage. We don't know quite what it means. What's more, learning a little more about the holiday Twelfth Night raises more questions rather than nailing down historical meanings. And that's a good beginning for thinking about how placing a play in the moment of its first performance complicates rather than simplifies its meaning. We have to ask what 'Twelfth

Night' could mean. But the answers we find are not definitive. History doesn't clear things up or fix meanings. It helps us see where the debates and contradictions are; it helps us think about what's at stake even in comedies.

Periodization

First a word about what we call the time when *Twelfth Night* was first performed. The question of how we divide up and name the past is often called 'periodization'. Historians and literary critics use several different terms for the period we will be discussing in this book. Simplest and least freighted is to call it 'sixteenth- and seventeenth-century England'. But that's a mouthful. The most familiar term is probably the Renaissance. The word 'renaissance' means 'rebirth'. The period is named for the rebirth of classical learning, as scholars rediscovered the ideas, literature and art of antiquity. In Europe, the Renaissance began in the late fourteenth century. But in England, what is sometimes called a Renaissance began almost a century later. The English Renaissance is often said to begin with the Tudor dynasty – Henry VIII's father, Henry VII, who took the throne in 1485 – and then end during the English civil wars when King Charles I was beheaded in 1649. What we call the Renaissance was, then, a very long period. What's more, many people did not have a 'Renaissance', because the rediscovery of classical learning would not have mattered to or even registered with the uneducated. Still, Renaissance remains an appealing and useful term for the flourishing of learning, artistic expression and innovation many see in the fifteenth, sixteenth and seventeenth centuries.

Historians usually call this period the 'early modern'. Some people object that this term serves to annex the period as the precursor to the modern era, our own. A reviewer once snidely described a history of early modern marriage and family as 'the history of us'. However, the term 'early modern' is not always invested in a progress narrative that leads to ourselves. It is often used, instead, to describe the many aspects of life that do not change that rapidly – that is, continuity rather than dramatic change, stasis rather than progress. For many historians, the usefulness of the term is that it covers a broad expanse of time, often 1500–1800. While many who use the term are not invested in claiming the period as the precursor to modernity, it is worth considering the charge that it is somehow wrong to think about how the past impinges on our own lives. Shakespeare did not look forward, anticipating and preparing for us. But in looking backward, we can't help but look from our own vantage point, bearing our own concerns, anxieties and investments.

It is important to be aware of anachronism, which means, literally, 'backwards time' or being out of step with time. The term usually describes an inability or failure to grasp the difference between past and present. It would be an anachronism if the characters in *Downton Abbey* were all using mobile phones and laptop computers. But you should keep in mind that the sixteenth- and seventeenth-century theatre depended on anachronism, dressing ancient Roman senators, Egyptian queens and fourteenth-century kings in clothing contemporary to the audience not the period being depicted. Imposing our own vocabulary, concerns or assumptions onto the past is often disparaged as anachronism. But the fear of anachronism can also be an excuse to avoid topics we were once told did not pertain to the past. I remember being told, for instance, that there was little racial difference in sixteenth- and seventeenth-century England, so raising the issue of race would be 'anachronistic'. Yet, as soon as scholars began to ask questions about racial and ethnic difference, we began to see it. As it turns out, there was abundant difference in the period, even if the vocabulary used to describe it was not always the one we use. A student who wonders why 'Ethiope' or 'Jew' is used as an insult in Shakespeare already knows that racial and ethnic difference – and prejudice – existed in his world and linger in his language. So the injunction not to bring up race was motivated by anxiety about a vexed topic in the present, not its irrelevance in the past.

Finally, people often use individuals to sum up historical periods. I've mentioned the Tudors. Five members of this family ruled England from 1485 to 1603. The recent television show about this dynasty has heightened awareness of them. Elizabeth I is the most famous member of the family and the most often represented in historical fiction, television and film, on t-shirts, mugs and other souvenirs. In a line-up of British sovereigns in a wax museum, Elizabeth I (and her father Henry VIII) are among the monarchs most people would be likely to recognize. Elizabeth had a long reign, from 1558 to 1603. She was also, it has been argued, a highly visible presence even in an age without mass media. Many of her subjects would have known what she looked like. However, dividing time by monarchs grants the monarchy enormous power to define an era and may give kings and queens more cultural importance than they deserve. It also obscures the ways that, when a leader dies, subjects live on. This habit of dividing time by monarchs has made it hard to name the fabulous if short-lived experiment in doing without a monarchy in England. This is often called 'the interregnum', or the time between kings, demonstrating how hard it is to imagine and name a period without a monarch. Another problem with the terms 'Elizabethan' or 'Tudor' to describe Shakespeare's era is that *Twelfth Night* was written at the end of Elizabeth's reign; Shakespeare's late plays were performed after Elizabeth died and after the Tudor dynasty ended and the Stuart dynasty began.

People sometimes use the categories 'Shakespeare's England' or 'Shakespeare's era'. In some ways, this makes sense, because we are organizing our inquiry into the past around him and his works. For us, the England he lived in was his and attracts our attention because it was his. But while this makes sense, perhaps, in a Shakespeare class, it starts to fall apart when we shift our attention elsewhere in the curriculum or textbook. Wasn't it also Spenser's and Sidney's and Jonson's and Milton's England? Why do we so seldom give a woman writer the power to define an era (at least before Jane Austen!)? The world of the theatre was highly collaborative, with playwrights working together, and many hands, including those of censors and actors, shaping performances. To set one author apart and above this collaboration is to downplay or even cover up a more interesting story about Shakespeare. This story is not about whether Shakespeare really wrote his plays. He did. It is about collaboration, close friendships and professional rivalries among men; managing a theatre company and getting ahead; appealing to patrons and playing to audiences; borrowing and learning from peers. If anything, theatre was more like the writers' room for sitcoms or the rivalry, collaboration and ambition of dotcom startups than the lonely garret of the starving artist we sometimes imagine.

I don't mean to confuse you. But just as I will draw your attention to choices you make and their implications – Viola or Cesario, she or he; verbs you'll use to describe the relationship between the play and another text – so I want you to be aware that there are a range of terms available and that while you can use any you might want to think about your choice. Students often use terms for historical periods interchangeably, as if any one will work to refer to 'back in the day'. But Medieval and Victorian are not the same. And the period we will be discussing here is neither Medieval nor Victorian but falls between the two. So be mindful when you choose a term. I will use the term 'early modern' as well as more specific references to 'sixteenth- and seventeenth-century' England.

Starting with when and where

One strategy I'd like to suggest to you as you work through the play and through this book is that you use the play as a starting point – as evidence in itself – rather than turning first to the work of historians and critics to explain it. A question to ask yourself as you read the play is: if you had only this play as your evidence what would you think you knew about early modern England? Each reader will have a different answer. This question invites you to think about how the play presents itself to us as evidence and conveys a vivid impression of social life, even as it announces that its setting is fantastical, that its time is somewhat outside of history.

You can start getting your bearings as a journalist might, asking when? and where? How does the play locate itself in time and place? One of the things directors first decide when mounting a production is where and when they'll set it. So we can have a *Twelfth Night* set in late nineteenth-century Europe (in Trevor Nunn's 1996 film) or in twenty-first century London (in Tim Supple's 2003 film). What does the play itself tell you about its time and place? In part, directors have some flexibility because the time and place are vague. The title refers to time, to a particular night, yet it is hard to pin down precisely when this is. Would Shakespeare's audience have recognized this as their 'now'? Do you? At the start of the second scene, the Captain informs a bewildered Viola that 'This is Illyria'. But where is that? Shakespeare is notoriously fanciful about place, giving Bohemia a seacoast in *The Winter's Tale*, for instance. The name 'Illyria' evokes words like illusion and lyrical, suggesting that it is an early version of fantasy places such as Neverland, Wonderland, or Oz. On the other hand, scholars have pointed out that Illyria was a real place on early modern maps, part of the Adriatic coast associated with the threat of shipwrecks and piracy (Pentland). Many critics also assume that, at some level, Shakespeare's plays are always set in a version of England or at least comment on English events and values. But if plays like *Twelfth Night* comment on Shakespeare's England, they do so through distancing and distortion. That's why placing the plays in an historical context is such a slippery but rewarding process. Its time defined by a holiday and its setting vague, the play advises us that historical accuracy is not its game.

Mapping the characters

The next question after where and when is who. Rather than list characters individually, it is most useful, I think, to map out how you think characters might be grouped. There is no one correct strategy for doing this and each strategy affords fresh insights into the relationships among characters. Who goes with whom? One obvious strategy is to divide the characters in terms of Orsino's and Olivia's households. In some of Shakespeare's romantic comedies, the characters move to an unfamiliar space of possibility, often a forest, which has sometimes been called a 'green world' (Frye 182–4). In *Twelfth Night*, in contrast, while Viola and Sebastian go to a new place, we never see them elsewhere, nor do they ever mention wishing to return to their home; Illyria is the only setting the play shows us. Orsino and Olivia stay where they are and ultimately incorporate the newcomers into their homes. Their households are thus the key settings for the play and the means of organizing the characters into communities.

Recent scholarship has drawn our attention to the fact that early modern households were not organized only around blood ties or marriage. Households were capacious and included many kinds of intimacy. Duke Orsino's household includes only men, but among them we find a range of 'Lords' or friends, servants, musicians – and Cesario, of whom Orsino promptly can say 'I have unclasped/ To thee the book even of my secret soul' (1.4.13–14). In her household, Olivia has a female servant, Maria, a male steward, Malvolio (who would manage the finances of her household and estate), a clown, Feste, various servants, and a kinsman, Sir Toby Belch. Malvolio explains to Toby: 'though she harbours you as her kinsman she's nothing allied to your disorders. If you can separate yourself and your misdemeanours, you are welcome to the house. If not … she is very willing to bid you farewell' (2.3.94–9). There is also Sir Toby's friend, Sir Andrew Aguecheek, whom Toby seems to be stringing along and bilking for money on the promise of helping him land Olivia as a wife. Contrasting the two households reveals who is missing. While many Shakespearean comedies include parents (most often fathers) as blocking figures – that is, as obstacles to their children's romances and independence – here there is no older generation except for Sir Toby, who depends on Olivia rather than wielding authority over her. The play tells us explicitly that Olivia's and Viola's and Sebastian's fathers are dead. It makes no mention of their mothers, presumably so long gone that they are forgotten rather than mourned and do not even merit mention. These young people are all free to make their own choices and matches.

Mapping the characters makes it easier to consider what the plot accomplishes or changes for those characters. Who is divided from whom? Who is brought together? For instance, thinking in terms of these households might remind us that, in the course of the plot, the two households are united for a double wedding. They aren't joined by Orsino's and Olivia's marriage, as we might expect at the start of the play, but by the householders' marriages to the twins, Viola and Sebastian. At the end of the play, Olivia appeals to Orsino 'To think me as well a sister as a wife, / One day shall crown th'alliance on't, so please you, / Here at my house and at my proper cost' (5.1.311–13). Olivia thus proposes to gather most of the cast into her house and to pay the bill. At one level, she asserts domestic and economic authority. Claiming kinship with Orsino, after evading him throughout the play, she takes the upper hand as the head of this new conjoined family. But power can also be a limitation. Thinking in terms of households reveals that Olivia, even as she abandons her resolve to stay confined to her household once she falls for Cesario, never really leaves it. Olivia stays rooted in her own household and can only respond to what comes to her. Cesario, in contrast, is a particularly mobile character, able to move from household to household. But he is also more exposed. Focusing on households also highlights those few characters who can't quite be accommodated by this organization (including Antonio and the Captain).

We might divide the men from the women – which reveals how few women there are, comparatively, especially since one, Viola, is a man for most of the play. If we think in terms of who seems to belong together, we might start to pair characters both by and across gender, even if those couplings don't last for the course of the play and even if they have varying meanings. Orsino insists that he and Olivia belong together, but textual evidence says otherwise. Olivia and Orsino do not meet face to face until the conclusion of the play. Of course, another important pair, the twins Viola and Sebastian, do not really meet until the end of the play either. Approaching the question of who belongs together in terms of who shares the stage, we will quickly identify these couples: Antonio and Sebastian; Orsino and Cesario; Olivia and Cesario (who is then replaced with his lookalike Sebastian).

Many Shakespeare comedies include close friendships between women. Does this play? Although Olivia and her servant Maria have interchangeable handwriting, and Maria clearly voices Olivia's authority to others, the play does not present them as friends or confidants. There is no scene, for example, in which Olivia confides to Maria about her feelings for Cesario. Furthermore, we never see Olivia with Viola, only with Cesario. Viola and Olivia's names are near anagrams of one another – that is, the two names contain the same letters with the addition of an 'I' for Olivia. (The letters in their names also link them to Malvolio.) Viola and Olivia are clearly a kind of pair. Each seems to find a mate. Each expresses more ardent desire for her eventual mate than he for her. But there are differences as well. Olivia actively pursues Sebastian while Viola waits for the circumstances to allow Orsino to see her as a potential spouse. Olivia chooses a man she meets as a servant and who agrees to be ruled by her. Viola chooses her master. They also both resemble male characters more than they do one another. For example, Viola is clearly paired with her twin, Sebastian, even though they rarely appear together on stage. Viola and Sebastian both cede agency and follow others' leads at the end of the play.

Various characters can be paired based on their resemblances. Maria and Viola both take on others' identities: Maria passes off her writing as her mistress Olivia's; Viola dresses as her brother to play Cesario. Cesario and Malvolio are alike in a range of ways, including being suitors to Olivia, servants, and opponents to and victims of the Sir Toby gang. Cesario praises Feste and in some ways also resembles him. Malvolio also resembles Orsino, in that both are suitors whom Olivia spurns. Echoes across the play draw attention to such resemblances. Cesario tells Orsino that if he fell in love with a woman, it would only be one 'Of your complexion' (2.4.26) and Malvolio remembers Olivia as saying that if she fell in love, 'it should be one of my complexion' (2.5.23–4). Just a scene apart, these lines invite us to compare Cesario's and Malvolio's attraction to their employers. Orsino does not recognize that his servant loves him; Malvolio mistakenly thinks that his mistress loves him. Cesario tells Olivia that if he wooed her in earnest, in his own cause, he would make her 'pity me' (1.5.268). He later responds to Olivia's outpouring of love for him by saying 'I pity you' (3.1.121), underscoring the reversal of roles by which she has become the spurned lover (Malcolmson 39). At the end of the play, Olivia refers to Malvolio as a 'poor fool' (5.1.363). While the fool Feste is one of his key tormentors, what might we learn about the play by thinking of these two as a pair?

Boy actors, cross-dressing and sexuality

Grouping characters can also alert us to the fact that gender is itself a question in the play and on the English stage in the sixteenth and seventeenth centuries. When we think about Shakespeare's plays in historical context or as documents of the period in which they were first performed, one of the first points to consider is that men and boys played all the roles, including women's parts. The boy actors who played women's parts worked until they were 19 or 20, so they weren't toddlers, and they served as apprentices, receiving board, room, clothing and training, rather than salary, similar to interns today. A boy actor would work up from minor parts such as pages to big roles such as Viola/Cesario (Belsey, 'Shakespeare's' 56). Some scholars speculate that a master-apprentice relationship might have influenced casting, so that a more experienced actor might be cast in a role in which he would often appear in scenes alone with his apprentice, a boy actor, and could help to coach him as they worked together, perhaps rehearsing more than the rest of the company would (McMillin).

As far as we know now, women did not write plays for public performance, nor did they act on public stages. (Keep in mind, however, that women did write plays to be read or for amateur performance in homes; they performed in a variety of venues, from entertainments at court to staged readings of plays in households; they did a great deal of the work on which the playhouse depended, including making costumes [Korda]; and they attended the theatre as spectators.) The meaning of this theatrical convention has been much disputed. But before you can enter that conversation you have to wrap your mind around the idea that there were no women on Shakespeare's stage. In England, women actors did not take speaking parts on the professional stage until the late seventeenth century. Was this simply a convention so familiar that contemporaries hardly thought about it? What about the fact that Shakespeare draws our attention to cross-dressing by having heroines such as Viola dress up as men? While critics have long discussed the dizzying layering this creates – when a boy plays a young woman who then dresses as a boy – the question remains as to what audiences made of it. One thing we know is that audience members did not all respond in the same way. Some might have given this familiar convention little thought. Some might have been aroused by the boy dressed as a girl dressed as a boy. Others might have been alarmed by the fluid attractions and attachments this common theatrical practise encouraged and on which the plots focus; certainly some attacks on the theatre critique it precisely for provoking unsettling desires. What evidence does the play itself offer us about what transvestism means in the period? What evidence does it provide about attitudes toward gender, sexuality and clothing?

Many of the most influential and insightful critics of *Twelfth Night* in the last few decades have focused on transvestism and homoeroticism (which means attraction between members of the same sex) in the play. While the stage relied upon boys dressed as women (as well as low-status men dressed as kings and white men in black face) the cross-dressing at the centre of this play's plot reverses the daily transformation on which the theatre depended; rather than a boy dressed as a woman, we see a woman dressed as a young man. Debate centres on the sexuality of the twins, Viola/Cesario and Sebastian, whose arrival in Illyria kick-starts the play. C. L. Barber presents this process as magical or mythical: 'Orsino and Olivia are languishing in melancholy until out of the sea comes an ambiguous figure "that can sing both high and low," who eventually becomes male to Olivia and female to Orsino, and so crystallizes the comic society' (Barber 83). We might also describe Viola's entrance into Illyrian society more prosaically. Of noble birth but suddenly alone in the world, Viola chooses a male disguise because she cannot work in Olivia's household (because Olivia is in mourning) and cannot be employed as a woman in a bachelor's household (or so she seems to suggest). She is a woman with, she thinks, no male relatives at all. Although she dons breeches to find work, she never presents this work as a matter of economic need (see Dowd). She has no trouble paying the Captain, for instance, and spurns tips and gifts when they are offered to her. The play presents her as freely choosing to enter one of these households as a servant, rather than as driven by economic need. Her role as a servant appears temporary from the start, rather than a permanent change in her identity. She waits in service so that she 'might not be delivered to the world – / Till

I had made mine own occasion mellow – / What my estate is' (1.2.39–41). Mellow functions here both as an adjective modifying occasion and in an adverbial clause describing the change she hopes time will achieve. Punctuation can alter the sense, attaching mellow either back to occasion or forward to the last clause. But what will it mean to mellow her occasion or her estate? The point is that Viola does not seek a salary by which to earn a new social identity. Instead, she seeks to prepare herself in less concrete ways. Not yet ready for prime time, Viola depicts her work as a servant as a time out, during which she will wait until she can deliver herself to the world, that is, as a kind of pregnancy that will result in the birth of her new self. As it happens, the plot delivers her not through her own ripeness or mellowness as much as through outside events. Finding her brother, revealing her identity, and receiving a marriage proposal combine to deliver her to the world.

Viola cannot present herself in her own garb as a potential employee because, as the Captain explains, Olivia 'will admit no kind of suit' (1.2.42). Viola must, then, don a suit. If the disguise serves the plot, placing Cesario in Orsino's house and on intimate terms with him and sending Cesario into Olivia's house as a suitor, Viola also expresses unease about the deception inherent in disguise (and in theatricality). She says to the captain:

> … though that nature with a beauteous wall
> Doth oft close in pollution, yet of thee
> I will believe thou hast a mind that suits
> With this thy fair and outward character. (1.2.45–8)

Here 'suits' means 'fits'; the captain's mind 'suits' his fair appearance. Viola proposes 'such disguise as haply shall become / The form of my intent' (1.2.51–2). What precisely does this mean? She proposes that mind and outward character, form and intent can conjoin for her as they do for the Captain. Clothes will make the man and provide a suitable outward form for Viola's intentions. Yet she is also embarking on disguise, a kind of deception about which she later expresses unease.

There is also a loose thread in this scene. Viola proposes that the Captain should present her to Orsino 'as an eunuch' (1.2.53). Meaning what? According to the gloss in most editions, this means a 'castrato', that is, a young man whose testicles have been removed. The name Cesario might even refer to this. Cesario means belonging to Caesar, which might mark Cesario as the possession or beloved of a leader (or duke). But the name Caesar itself might derive from the Latin word for 'cut' because he was born by what is still called 'Caesarean section', or what Shakespeare describes in *Macbeth* as being from the mother's womb 'untimely ripped' (*Macbeth* 5.10.16; Orgel 53–4). However, after Viola proposes this, she never mentions it again. Cesario might, for example, advise Olivia that he is a eunuch so as to thwart her erotic interest in him but he does not.

Everyone who describes Cesario emphasizes his androgyny, that is, the way that he combines feminine and masculine qualities. Orsino, for instance, proposes that Olivia will be more receptive to Cesario than to an adult male messenger. 'It shall become thee well to act my woes./ She will attend it better in thy youth/ Than in a nuncio's of more grave aspect' (1.4.26–8). In Orsino's view, Cesario's advantage is more than youth.

> For they shall yet belie thy happy years
> That say thou art a man. Diana's lip
> Is not more smooth and rubious. Thy small pipe
> Is as the maiden's organ, shrill and sound,
> And all is semblative a woman's part. (1.4.30–4)

'Semblative' means here similar to or resembling. Then as now, the word 'part' can refer to a body part – so that the woman's part would be female genitals – or a part in a play – so that the woman's part is a female role. The phrase thus gestures to both the body and roleplaying as determining gender. In saying that everything about Cesario resembles a woman's part, Orsino also opens up the difference between resembling a woman's part and having or playing one. Orsino's praise is part of his explanation of why Olivia would receive or prefer Cesario as a messenger. Critics dispute whether Olivia admits Cesario because he is 'unthreatening' (Moglen 16) or because he is deferential, and 'specifically acknowledges Olivia's position in relation to his' (Giese 71). Barber claims that Olivia, being a 'spoiled and dominating young heiress', might have been drawn to Cesario's softness because she wants to be the dominant partner in a relationship (Barber 244). She does, after all, express her hope that Cesario/Sebastian will 'be ruled by me' (4.1.63). (Earlier, she also expresses a willingness to 'buy' Cesario's affection and leads with an expensive present: 'How shall I feast him? What bestow of him? / For youth is bought more oft than begged or borrowed' [3.4.2–3].)

Malvolio describes Cesario as,

> Not yet old enough for a man nor young enough for a boy; as a squash is before 'tis a peasecod, or a codling when 'tis almost an apple. 'Tis with him in standing water, between boy and man. He is very well-favoured and he speaks very shrewishly. One would think his mother's milk were scarce out of him. (1.5.152–7)

Orsino and Malvolio, interestingly, Olivia's two suitors, both see Cesario as both masculine and feminine, both child and adult. What we might call 'effeminacy' is associated with youth here, with being high voiced and smooth cheeked. At the same time, Viola and Sebastian both remark on Cesario's resemblance to Sebastian (2.1.23–4). Viola/Cesario marvels:

>   I my brother know
> Yet living in my glass. Even such and so
> In favour was my brother, and he went
> Still in this fashion, color, ornament,
> For him I imitate. (3.4.376–80)

Since they were dressed alike, and both played by boy actors, Cesario and Sebastian might have been difficult for spectators to tell apart, thus adding to the confusions around identity in the play. Careful attention to descriptions of Cesario and Sebastian uncovers the gender ambiguity and fluid erotic attractions in *Twelfth Night*. Either Olivia is attracted to a womanish man or Orsino to a mannish woman. Or both.

In this book, I call the character Viola/Cesario or simply Cesario after the second scene in which we see Viola in her maiden's weeds, because that's how other characters know him. Starting with the First Folio, the speech prefixes in most editions, that is, the labels that tell you which character says what, consistently identify Viola as Viola. This suggests a continuity of identity – Viola is always Viola – that the plot disrupts. For the other characters, Viola isn't Viola but Cesario. Her name is not uttered until Sebastian says it in the final scene. Even then, he says that he would only call Cesario Viola 'were' she a woman; Orsino continues to call his page and prospective wife Cesario and says he'll do so until he is dressed as she (Viola) (Jones and Stallybrass 199). So on stage, if you didn't know the play or have a programme identifying her as Viola, you would know the character only as Cesario. This simple choice of name and gendered pronoun – Cesario … he – carries implications. You are free to make a different choice, such as Viola/she or Cesario s/he. But you should make it self-consciously and explain your logic to your own readers. Be forewarned. No choice will resolve gender ambiguity or allow you to evade the same-sex attractions in this play. If this character is, for you, consistently Viola, then Olivia falls for a woman. And Sebastian looks like one.

It can be useful to contrast the relationships in the play revolving around mistaken gender identity to the attachment between Antonio and Sebastian. Each knows the other is a man. The words 'heterosexuality' and 'homosexuality' were coined in the nineteenth century. Arguably, these categories did not exist as we understand them in Shakespeare's time. That doesn't mean that sex between members of the same gender never occurred. The play itself suggests how easy it was to imagine and represent same-sex attachments. To say that the words 'heterosexual' and 'homosexual' did not exist is simply to acknowledge that that vocabulary, familiar to us now, was not available to Shakespeare and his contemporaries and that the habit of dividing people up by straight or gay, by what is now called 'object choice', was not yet well-established. Absent that system of categorization, the play itself suggests, attractions and attachments between members of the same sex simply took their place beside those between members of the opposite sexes. One might be drawn to a man and a woman, as Orsino and Sebastian both appear to be, without earning a particular identity label or experiencing those desires as a conflict.

By the end of 2.1, Antonio vows to follow Sebastian to Illyria, even though he faces imprisonment and prosecution there: 'But come what may I do adore thee so / That danger shall seem sport, and I will go' [to Illyria] (2.1.43–4). We don't really learn the basis of this adoration until the last scene of the play, when Antonio explains that he and Sebastian have been inseparable for the three months since he saved Sebastian's life. (This is the same period during which Cesario has lived with Orsino, a period described as days, so the twins seem to experience time differently.) Antonio explains that he was drawn to follow Sebastian, despite the danger to himself, because of 'jealousy what might befall your travel' (3.3.8). Many editors and critics have been in a hurry to distinguish this jealousy from sexual jealousy, insisting that Antonio simply expresses anxiety for Sebastian's safety. As the critic Valerie Traub asks: 'why do editors gloss "jealousy" as anxiety, when both words were available to Shakespeare, and both scan equally well?' (*Desire* 134). And what is the danger Antonio discounts because of his jealousy? Although he claims not to be a pirate, Antonio was in a sea fight with Orsino's galleys in which Orsino's nephew was injured; Antonio then refused to pay recompense for 'what we took from them' (that is booty) as the rest of his city did. When the officers first approach him in Illyria, he attempts to deny his identity

– 'You do mistake me, sir' (3.4.325) – but even in this play of mistaken and transformed identities, he cannot escape who he is or the consequences of his actions: 'he knows I know him well' (328–9), one officer confirms to the other. When Orsino calls him 'notable pirate, thou salt-water thief' he counters that 'Antonio never yet was thief or pirate' (5.1.65, 70). Antonio is in many ways the ideal man in the play: active, brave, strong, and constant. And in choosing Sebastian, he is in no way deceived, as Orsino and Olivia both are, at some level, in their choices. What, then, should we make of how his love story ends? We'll return to this question in Chapter 4.

For now, let's think again about the question I asked above about transvestism: if this play were your only evidence regarding early modern attitudes toward sexuality, what would you conclude? Just as it is impossible to specify what our own culture (or your own family) thinks about sexuality, since varying views coexist, even within a single person, so it is impossible to generalize about an early modern attitude toward sexuality. We can sketch out some outlines. But because sexuality is often off the record and under the radar we need to engage in some creative speculation, just as historians of sexuality do. What can we know? And what can we conjecture? We know that it was a felony to engage in 'sodomy', which referred to any kind of sexual penetration other than vaginal intercourse. But the rate of prosecution and conviction was extremely low. (In contrast to sodomy, adultery and fornication, or heterosexual inter-course outside of marriage, were sins but not crimes. They were not subject to criminal penalties.) In the kind of households Olivia and Orsino head in the play, there was a low level of privacy and a high degree of intimacy. It would not have been unusual for master and servant to share a bed, for example, or for servants to share beds with one another. Various forms of sexual expression that did not lead to pregnancy or attract too much attention seem to have been passed over as unremarkable.

Insults often yield illuminating insight into cultural values. In early modern slang, we find few insults that impugn men's masculinity in terms of their attraction or attractiveness to other men; insults instead focus on a wife's fidelity – describing the man whose wife has cheated on him as a cuckold – or a man's cowardice. The play depicts Antonio, who loves another man and is willing to fight for him, as more manly than Sir Andrew, who courts a woman, but is fearful and inept at combat. When Andrew faces off against Cesario in a duel, they're both playing men. In Shakespeare's *As You Like It*, Rosalind comments on the fact that even some men have to put on manliness: 'We'll have a swashing and a martial outside, / As many other mannish cowards have, / That do outface it with their semblances' (1.3.118–20).

While sodomy could include a range of practises, there was no comparable word to describe sexual congress between women in England. It seems to have been difficult for people in the period to count any act that did not involve a penis and penetration as sex. When Viola expresses concern that Olivia has fallen in love with her – 'Poor lady, she were better love a dream' (2.2.26) – she articulates the view that love between women is 'thriftless', impossible to translate into action. This is partly because she doesn't love Olivia in return but partly because, according to Viola, Olivia is 'mistaken' (35). C. L. Barber, an enormously influential critic of Shakespeare's comedies whose masterwork, *Shakespeare's Festive Comedy* was first published in 1959, explains that, in his view, this 'mistake' cannot be put right until Olivia mistakes Sebastian for Cesario. What Viola 'lacks', he assures us, 'Sebastian has' (246). Barber asserts his own view as self-evident, the simple truth of gender and sexuality. It is a truth universally acknowledged that a woman needs a penis. To fall for another woman is to make a mistake, to be a 'poor lady' destined for disappointment. But is Barber correct that this is the way of 'nature' or of the play?

Attitudes toward sexuality are not only subjective but change over time. We've seen enormous changes recently in attitudes toward same-sex marriage in Europe and the United States, for example. Ways of discussing sexuality in Shakespeare's plays have changed both because critics less often hold forth confidently about nature and norms, as

Barber once did, and because our understanding of early modern gender and sexuality has deepened so that it is harder to make bold and simplistic generalizations. For instance, Barber, from whom we just heard above, insists that the play affirms heteronormativity or the presumption that nature favours relationships between the sexes. 'Jack shall have Jill and nought shall go ill', as Shakespeare puts it in *A Midsummer Night's Dream*. But everything that Barber claims is indisputable in the play more recent critics and historians have cast into doubt. Barber claims that

> The most fundamental distinction the play brings home to us is the difference between men and women ... Just as a saturnalian reversal of social roles need not threaten the social structure, but can serve instead to consolidate it, so a temporary, playful reversal of sexual roles can renew the meaning of the normal relation. One can add that with sexual as with other relations, it is when the normal is secure that playful aberration is benign. This basic security explains why there is so little that is queazy in all Shakespeare's handling of boy actors playing women, and playing women pretending to be men. (245)

Mightn't we also interpret the play as revealing that the difference between men and women is not fundamental but rather unstable and manufactured? This is, after all, a play in which men play all three female characters and one female character passes as a man. Embedded in this passage from Barber is the judgement that heterosexuality is 'the normal relation', that alternatives to that normal relation are not only abnormal but 'aberrant' (and not necessarily in a 'benign' way), and that same-sex eroticism can make onlookers 'queazy'. Barber sees between Antonio and Sebastian 'one of those ardent attachments between young people of the same sex which Shakespeare frequently presents, with his positive emphasis, as exhibiting the loving and lovable qualities later expressed in love for the other sex' (246). In other words, friendship prepares young people for marriage, which then supersedes the friendship. While it is true that Shakespeare often depicts same-sex friendship leading up to marriage – between Cesario and Orsino, for instance – it is not a given that marriage replaces or cancels out that same-sex attachment. The plays often leave open the possibility that same-sex attachments and marriage can coexist and even support one another (Crawford). For example, critic Carol Neely points out that, at the end of the play, 'Sebastian remains loved by Antonio and Olivia and Viola and loves all three' (120).

In addition to the play's emphasis and reflections on cross-dressing and role playing, it is highly self-conscious about its status as a play. For example, when Cesario first visits Olivia, he alerts us to how hard it is to memorize one's part. 'I would be loath to cast away my speech, for, besides that it is excellently well penned, I have taken great pains to con [or memorize] it' (1.5.167–9). He explains that he can't answer a question that falls 'out of my part' (1.5.174). He is, he insists, simply playing the part Orsino has given him, just as all of the actors on stage are simply playing the parts they have been assigned in the play. With its acute awareness of how we perform ourselves in the world through clothes, demeanor and 'parts', all of which we can alter, the play draws our attention to its status as theatre and to our own embeddedness in theatricality. While it gestures toward historically particular practises – boy actors cross-dressing to play women's roles or the division of a play into 'parts' – its awareness of the world as a stage also extends beyond those specifics.

Queen Elizabeth I

Another way we might think about the play's place in history is in terms of its status as Elizabethan – that is, as a play performed during the reign of Queen Elizabeth I. *Twelfth Night* seems to have been written in 1601, when Elizabeth I was 68 years old. Since she died in 1603, she was at the end of her very long reign. If students know one English monarch before Victoria, it is probably Elizabeth because of her long afterlife in popular culture. Elizabeth was the daughter of Henry VIII and Anne Boleyn. Her father divorced his first wife (of some 24 years) to marry Anne, who was already pregnant with Elizabeth when they married. But then just a few years later, he had Anne executed on charges of adultery and incest; he also disowned his daughter Elizabeth. He went on to marry four more wives, and to behead another one of them. This is an unusually scandalous and therefore well-known history. As a consequence, people love to speculate as to its consequences for Elizabeth, still popularly known as the Virgin Queen because she never married. Surely she saw what marriage meant for her mother and stepmothers – beheaded, died, divorced, beheaded, survived (barely) – and decided that marriage was not for her. But it is impossible to know how Elizabeth made sense of her own family history or all of the reasons why she ultimately declined to marry.

There were at least as many political reasons as personal ones to postpone and ultimately refuse marriage. None of the available suitors was exactly right and, as contemporaries acknowledged, the queen would lose more than she would gain by marriage. This was the case because of the widespread insistence that men were superior to women and thus more suited to rule and that husbands inevitably and appropriately dominated their wives. As queen, Elizabeth held power alone. If she married, that would always be under negotiation and in doubt – as it was not for a king like her father when he married. She is famously credited with monopolizing a whole range of vocabularies and gender roles as it suited her, presenting herself as a loving mother, a wife married to her country, a remote, idealized and beloved mistress, a goddess, a prince or King. It is possible that she never said some of the remarks most widely attributed to her. But she does seem to have self-consciously emphasized her ability to combine attributes associated with both men and women, kings and queens. As she appears to have said in one famous speech on a battlefield: 'I know I have the body but of a weak and feeble woman, but I have the heart and stomach of a king, and of a king of England too' (Tudor 326). As a composite of male and female, a couple in herself, Elizabeth did not need to marry.

One critic, Leah Marcus, connects the queen's claim to be simultaneously male and female to the cross-dressed heroines of Shakespeare's comedies late in the queen's reign, including *Twelfth Night*.

> The dramatic construct of a boy clothed as a woman, an altogether credible woman, who then expands her identity through male disguise in such a way as to mirror the activities which would be appropriate to her actual, hidden male identity – that construct precisely replicates visually the composite self-image the Queen created ... through language. (Marcus 101)

Marcus's argument draws attention to what happens to the heroines in the plays: they marry as the queen never did. In their conclusions, Marcus argues, Shakespeare's plays undo the fantasy of Elizabeth's composite identity: unlike the queen, heroines like Viola 'cannot permanently sustain the self-sufficiency of their composite natures, but must go out and get themselves husbands – something it was obviously too late for Elizabeth herself to do' (Marcus 103). Viola must surrender her male costume and the freedoms of movement and expression it enables in order to be embraced as wife and sister. Marcus suggests that such an ending could be seen to discipline the queen as well as the character Viola by imposing marriage as the end of her androgynous independence. But this also reminds us that this surrender, for Viola, is anticipated but not enacted before our eyes. It is a maybe.

Shakespeare's comedies tend to end in marriage, for some if not for all. Marriage remains a shorthand for happy endings, however much our own knowledge and experience of marriage might challenge this set of assumptions. But we should not take this generic habit as a description of social life. Since all women did not get married in Shakespeare's England, we need not assume that comedies end with marriage for women just because that is somehow how it was or how it had to be. So we can ask: if not all women married in the period, if the most powerful woman in the country did not, how do we interpret the fact that all three female characters in *Twelfth Night* marry or plan to marry at the end? How do we feel about those marriages as rewards? What is gained or lost? Do we as readers or spectators make distinctions among the marriages?

Considering all of the marriages at the end of *Twelfth Night* might lead us to think about possible connections between Elizabeth and Olivia as well as Viola. Olivia and Viola both have, they think, a dead father and brother, as Elizabeth also did, making her all the sons of her father's house. (Elizabeth's dead mother, Anne Boleyn, was notorious. Olivia's is never mentioned.) Olivia is the most independent and powerful woman of the three female characters in the play. She is a Countess and the head of her own household. Linking Olivia to Elizabeth leads us to notice not just her independence and authority but also the possibility that she prepares to surrender them in marriage (as Elizabeth never did). If Olivia is a figure for Elizabeth, then it becomes noteworthy that, in contrast to the Virgin Queen, who was cautious and hesitant regarding marriage and engaged in several protracted courtships that never resulted in wedlock, Olivia marries 'with remarkable and uncharacteristic alacrity, incaution and hopefulness' (Mallin 193). Dympna Callaghan points to a similarity between the desire Sir Toby attributes to Olivia – 'She'll not match above her degree, neither in estate, years, nor wit – I have heard her swear't' (1.3.105–7) – and various accounts of Elizabeth I's reluctance to marry a spouse who might eclipse her power in some way: 'initially, this resolution seems synonymous with the desire not to marry at all. For it seems inconceivable that Olivia would eschew marriage *up* the ladder of social hierarchy out of a desire to marry several rungs *down* it' (Callaghan, *Who?* 157). If marriage threatened the wife with a loss of power and status, there were two possible solutions to the problem. One was marrying down, as Olivia appears to do, so as to maintain the upper hand in marriage. After all, Sebastian agrees to be ruled by Olivia. The other solution was marrying across, choosing a spouse who is of equal status, age, and abilities. There are stories suggesting that Queen Elizabeth jokingly entertained the possibility of marrying another queen. We might read Olivia's attraction to a disguised Viola as another solution to the problem of finding a spouse who could be her equal and would not domineer over her. As one critic puts it, '*Twelfth Night* lets the queen figuratively woo and marry herself' (Mallin 203). We need not assume that only one of the heroines in the play can refer to Queen Elizabeth. Perhaps they both do.

Linking Olivia to Elizabeth helps us think about the question of whether the plot rewards or disciplines Olivia. Critics have disagreed. Some critics argue that the play's plot works to discipline Olivia, leading her to surrender her vow to cloister herself for seven years and her independent control over her own household and to marry a man who, at some level, she doesn't know. Jean Howard, for example, argues that the play presents Olivia as a more threatening figure than Viola: 'the play seems to me to applaud a cross-dressed woman who does not aspire to the positions of power assigned men [Viola] and to discipline a non-cross-dressed woman who does [Olivia]' (112). Olivia is 'punished, comically but unmistakably, by being made to fall in love with the cross-dressed Viola' (Howard 114). Mary Thomas Crane emphasizes that the play depicts Olivia as both concerned to seal her house off from outsiders and as unable to do so.

> Olivia's attempt to keep suitors out leads to a proliferation of suits for her hand from within her household as well as from outside it, and her attempts to regulate suitable behavior on the part of its inhabitants lead to extreme and inappropriate behavior. (Crane 103)

Even her fool makes himself at home with Orsino as well as with her. Other critics emphasize that Olivia finds and fulfils her desire and asserts her power. Carol Neely points out that when Olivia proposes a marriage feast in her own house, she forces Orsino's hand, prompting him to propose marriage to Cesario. 'Hence the play that begins in the household of Orsino ends at Olivia's; she displaces the Duke as the primary authority figure in Illyria' (Neely 121).

A contemporary who saw a production of *Twelfth Night* offers us two ways of thinking about the connection between Olivia's independence and authority and Queen Elizabeth I. John Manningham, one viewer of a performance of the play in 1602, was a law student in London. In his diary, he described a performance of the play in February 1602, offering us what amounts to a very rare review of a seventeenth-century performance. (Newspapers as we now know them did not yet exist, nor of course did the other kinds of media on which we now rely. Although many people went to the theatre regularly, there was not yet a structure for formal review of performances. As a consequence, scholars treasure those rare informal mentions of performance – when one spectator such as Manningham has recorded his or her response to a play.) Manningham links the play to Plautus's ancient Roman play *Menaechmi* and Shakespeare's *Comedy of Errors*, both of which emphasize twins and mistaken identity (although both those sets of twins are the same sex). One of the most interesting details in Manningham's review is that he refers to Olivia as the steward's or Malvolio's 'Lady widowe'. Perhaps Manningham thought this because the character was dressed in black, or because Olivia has a widow's financial independence, or because many widows married their subordinates and this was a recognized way for men to improve their social and economic status. One of Shakespeare's sources appears to be the story of 'Apolonius and Silla' in Barnabe Riche's prose fiction *Riche his Farewell to Military Profession* (1581), based on Nicolo Secchi's 1547 play *Gl'Inganni* or *The Deceived* (for Shakespeare's sources, see Bullough). In this prose fiction, the Olivia character is a widow. Perhaps that shaped Manningham's expectations. At any rate, Manningham misremembered Olivia as a widow.

Manningham's diary does not relate to the play only through his comments on the performance he saw. The play makes one direct reference to a story about Elizabeth when Fabian says 'This is to give a dog and, in recompense, desire my dog again' (5.1.5–6). This refers to a popular story about the queen that Manningham records in his diary.

> Mr. Francis Curle told me how one Dr. Boleyn, the Queen's kinsman, had a dog which he doted on, so much that the Queen understanding of it requested he would grant her one desire, and he should have whatsoever he would ask. She demanded his dog; he gave it, and 'Now, Madame,' quoth he, 'you promised to give me my desire.' 'I will,' quoth she. 'Then I pray you give me my dog again' (Manningham's Diary 149, entry for March 1602/3)

Manningham recorded this story after the play's first performance and after the Queen had died. Fabian's reference to this story suggests that it circulated as gossip or urban legend for several years before Manningham recorded it. What makes it a memorable story? In part it is about getting 'what you will', which makes it seem relevant to the play. It depicts the queen as demanding but also tells a story about her comeuppance. She does not get what she wills, the dog, but is outsmarted by her kinsman, who is also her doctor and a courtier.

Malvolio and puritanism

Of all the play's characters, it is 'the steward' Manningham remembers. Of the play's action, he remarks not on double romances, disguise and duels in what is usually taken as the main plot but on the joke pulled on Malvolio in the subplot:

A good practise in it to make the steward believe his Lady widow was in Love with him, by counterfeiting a letter, as from his Lady, in general terms, telling him what she liked best in him, and prescribing his gesture in smiling, his apparel, &c., and then when he came to practise, making him believe they took him to be mad.

Why did Malvolio stand out for Manningham? According to one critic, scapegoating Malvolio 'allows him to scorn Puritans, distance himself from erotic intrigue and women's power, and disavow the marital/economic ambition he shares with Malvolio. He, like the tricksters, relishes "practises" that advance status by putdowns of opponents' (Neely 155). Evidence survives that others in the seventeenth and eighteenth centuries also saw Malvolio as the star, remembering the play as his vehicle. One of Shakespeare's contemporaries even complained that his own play was not as popular as Shakespeare's because he didn't have a Malvolio:

Had there appear'd some sharp cross-garter'd man
Whom their loud laugh might nick-name Puritan,
Cas'd up in factious breeches and small ruffe ...
Then sure they would have given applause to crown
That which their ignorance did now cry down. (Stern, Documents 87)

As this bitter poem attests, Malvolio was a memorable character, one audiences loved to ridicule.

We've talked about Elizabeth I as one figure for an historical world outside the play that may in some ways enter into or impinge on it. But Malvolio is often taken as a figure for history because of the fact that he is called a 'kind of puritan' (2.3.136). Although Puritans were often satirized on the stage, not everyone associated with the theatre was anti-Puritan nor were all Puritans anti-theatre. As we will see, the play itself undermines that simple opposition between Puritans and theatre. In the course of the sixteenth century, a protracted religious Reformation divided Protestants from Catholics. This Reformation had many causes and unfolded across many years. It crystallized when King Henry VIII announced a break from the pope in Rome and founded a new Church of England with himself as its head, demanding that his subjects view him as their spiritual as well as political leader. Catholics insisted that they could sustain an allegiance to the pope in Rome as well as the English monarch, while Protestants condemned such divided allegiances and vowed loyalty only to the monarch as both political leader and spiritual head. The Reformation extended and consolidated the sovereign's power and justified the seizure of the Church's considerable properties in England (monasteries and convents), which the King then redistributed as it served his own interests. Henry VIII had complex reasons for initiating this split, which gained particular urgency for him because the pope refused to grant him a divorce from his first wife so that he could marry a second, Anne Boleyn, who would be the mother of the future queen Elizabeth I. But this shift in England also participated in larger movements across Europe as members of the Catholic church derided its corruption, challenged its theology, and demanded change.

The sweeping changes that followed as a result of these 'protests' have come to be called the Reformation and the adherents of the newly reformed faith 'protestants'. Adherents of the two faiths disagreed about many things, including the role of images in worship, the meaning of the Eucharist (did it actually become Christ's body or did it just represent that body?), access to the Bible (which Protestants insisted should be translated into vernacular languages and placed in believers' own hands), the value of extra-scriptural custom (which Catholics valued and Protestants disdained), and the structure of the institutional church (which, in Catholicism, granted more authority to priests and relied on an elaborate hierarchy of pope, bishops, cardinals, and priests), and the value of a celibate clergy (which Catholics upheld and Protestants decried).

This was a paradigm-shifting, culture-shaking split within Christianity and the line between Catholic and Protestant remained a contested yet central one throughout the early modern period. The confusion and debate this change caused register in Shakespeare's plays in a range of ways, direct and indirect. For example, as we will see in the next chapter, the depiction of Olivia as vowing to confine herself 'like a cloistress' must be understood in the context of a culture that had shuttered convents (and their cloisters) and limited women's access to the nunnery as an alternative to marriage. But the conflicts were not only between Catholics and Protestants. Divisions within Protestantism soon proliferated. Those conflicts underpin the characterization of Malvolio in the play. First named by their detractors, Puritans represented the most extreme wing of Protestants, those who wanted reforms of liturgy and ecclesiastical structure to go even further. Like Catholics, they were subject to fines and imprisonment for their refusal to conform to Church of England practises. They were also suspected as civil dissidents. 'Puritans' figured importantly among those who left England to settle in the colonies. They sought greater religious freedom for themselves (but did not necessarily bring with them greater religious toleration for others).

In the play, Malvolio's character is presented more in terms of his self-love and self-importance than of any concrete religious beliefs. Sir Toby and the others hate him as a social climber and spoilsport. 'Art any more than a steward?' Sir Toby asks him. 'Dost thou think because thou art virtuous there shall be no more cakes and ale?' (2.3.112–13). 'Cakes and ale' were the conventional food of traditional church-sponsored festivities. So at one level Sir Toby defends his right to the kinds of pleasures associated with a 'merry England' before the Reformation, the world of maypoles, hobbyhorses, and other traditional games and sports. In his defence of pleasure, Sir Toby also anticipates later exponents of self-indulgence, such as the libertine (Appelbaum). Sir Toby associates Malvolio (whose name suggests ill will) with a whole raft of restrictions on the pleasures of life. So even as we consider why Malvolio seemed to be the star of the play for some viewers, we also need to think about why Sir Toby and others select him as 'the trout that must be caught with tickling' (2.5.19–20). We see him in action in 1.5 when he says to Olivia of Feste: 'Unless you laugh and minister occasion to him, he is gagged' (1.5.82–3). By stifling laughter and gagging the fool, he threatens the possibility of play in many ways. For this reason, he is a hard figure for theatre people to like. As a result, 'There is an all but universal convention for commentators to stand up and be counted as in favour of cakes and ale' (Berry 111) and to ignore the snobbish meanness of Toby's question preceding the one about cakes and ale: 'Art any more than a steward?' (2.3.112). In other words, who do you think you are? You are just a servant.

A faction we could call Puritan closed the London theatres in 1642. There followed civil war, regicide (the beheading of King Charles I) and the 'interregnum' or Protectorate, a remarkable period in which England did not have a ruling monarch. The theatres did not reopen until this upheaval, which was also a visionary experiment in governmental models other than monarchy, had ended when monarchy was 'restored'. When Charles II returned to England as its King, the theatres also re-opened. Why were the theatres closed in 1642? The 'Order for Stage-plays to cease' passed by Parliament read as follows:

...whereas public Sports do not well agree with public Calamities, nor public Stage-plays with the Seasons of Humiliation, this being an Exercise of sad and pious solemnity, and the other being Spectacles of pleasure, too commonly expressing lascivious Mirth and Levity: It is therefore thought fit, and Ordained by the Lords and Commons in this Parliament Assembled, that while these sad Causes and set times of Humiliation do continue, public Stage-plays shall cease, and be forborne. (Potter 61–2)

The proclamation expresses some disapproval of stage-plays for 'expressing lascivious [meaning lustful] mirth and levity' and for promoting pleasure rather than politics. But it also suggests that plays are more untimely than evil; they simply do not suit a time in which people are contemplating a serious change in their government and lives are on the line. There are various practical reasons why the theatre might be viewed as dangerous. First and foremost, it was a place where people congregated, which is always risky. The theatre companies were also associated with royalty. Shakespeare's company was known as 'the king's men'. Although many plays critiqued the aristocracy and monarchy, the fact that the theatres closed when conflict exploded between Charles I and his Parliament and reopened when his son was 'restored' to the throne confirms an association between the crown and the theatre that might have motivated those who opposed the king to shut the theatres down.

This is all oversimplified, of course, a potted history of a complicated sequence of events. What's more, it might seem odd to connect the play to an event that occurred 40 years after it was first performed. Why, then, have I tried your patience? It all comes back to Malvolio. When Malvolio exits at the end of *Twelfth Night*, saying he'll be revenged 'on the whole pack of you' (5.1.371), many critics have read this as a prophecy that Puritans would close the theatres. For example, C. L. Barber states that 'in the long run, in the 1640s, Malvolio *was* revenged on the whole pack of them' (Barber 257; see also Callaghan, *Shakespeare Without* 47–8). But since there were 'puritan' sympathies within the theatre community and theatrical impulses among Puritans, it is not clear that Malvolio can reliably hold down the job of being anti-theatrical. If we look more closely at this contention we'll see, not for the last time, that attending to history complicates rather than clarifies. But this is also an example of how looking more closely at the play, and being willing to re-read and look again, can lead us to challenge generalizations that critics continue to repeat without question.

Let's return to Manningham's review in his diary of the performance he saw. Manningham describes Maria's scheme as a 'practise' that 'prescribes' how the steward should act. These words draw our attention to the ways in which Maria's letter provides Malvolio with a script. This weakens distinctions among reading, writing and acting. To write a description of how Malvolio should act is to change how he does. Furthermore, Maria does not need to transform Malvolio into an actor because he is already a performer. When he enters the trap laid for him to find the forged letter in 2.5, Maria reports that 'He has been yonder i'the sun practicing behaviour to his own shadow this half-hour' (2.5.14–15). Just as the schemers will practise upon him, he has already been practising the part to which he aspires. His inclination in that direction makes him putty in their hands. As he enters he 'jets under his advanced plumes' as Fabian describes it (2.5.29) and is engaged in an elaborate fantasy that is a script, with him playing against Sir Toby and others – even if he doesn't know that they are hidden in the tree observing him as an audience. His reading of the letter is a performance for that audience, whether he knows it or not. The letter then provides him a new script, which he follows to the letter in subsequent scenes. Maria says 'I have dogged him like his murderer. He does obey every point of the letter that I dropped to betray him' (3.2.72–4). As a playwright, director, and spectator, she is remarkably brutal. 'You have not seen such a thing as 'tis. I can hardly forbear hurling things at him; I know my lady will strike him' (3.2.73–74). Fabian says of Malvolio: 'If this were played upon a stage now, I could condemn it as an improbable fiction' (3.4.123–4). The schemers repeatedly call this a 'device'. Sir Toby says 'I smell a device' and Sir Andrew concurs 'I have't in my nose too' (2.3.157–8). So while it's satisfying to imagine Malvolio as the voice of anti-theatricality – expelled from the play's community but also destined to return to end the cakes and ale decades later – he is also himself a performer. For many, over the centuries, he has proven to be the star of this show. Noticing that Malvolio is as theatrical as he is anti-theatrical is a good reminder that we should always test generalizations and assumptions – no matter how oft-repeated or even especially if oft-repeated – against the evidence of the play itself.

The 'practise' upon Malvolio ultimately attempts to convince him he is mad (2.5.187–8; 3.4.129). But here, too, although Malvolio is presented as a scapegoat, he is not as different or alien as he might at first appear. Malvolio says to Sir Topas, 'I am no more mad than you are' (4.2.47), insinuating that everyone is mad. Later, Sebastian wonders, 'Are all the people mad?' (4.1.126). Once Sebastian is caught up in Olivia's pursuit of him he remarks that she cannot be as crazy as she seems because 'if 'twere so / She could not sway her house, command her followers, / Take and give back affairs and their dispatch/ With such a smooth, discreet and stable bearing / As I perceive she does' (4.3.16–20). Sebastian then asks himself,

> What relish is in this? How runs the stream?
> Or I am mad or else this is a dream.
> Let fancy still my sense in Lethe steep:
> If it be thus to dream, still let me sleep. (4.1.59–62)

At the simplest level, Sebastian is wondering what is going on in Illyria and with Olivia. His word 'relish' evokes the sensual register of taste. His question about which way the stream runs (like the modern references to which way the wind is blowing) reminds us of the many ways in which the sea and water figure in this play. Where we would use an 'either … or' structure, Sebastian uses the more common early modern phrasing of 'or … or' to explore alternatives. The alternatives are not the ones he sees. Olivia's interest in him is neither madness (in him or in her) nor a dream. Olivia herself later describes it as 'a most extracting frenzy of my own' (5.1.277), that is, a desire so intense that it distracted her so that she did not notice what was happening in her household with regard to the trick on Malvolio. Her word 'extracting', which

Shakespeare only uses in this unusual way once, might also suggest that her desire lifted her out of herself, just as one might extract an essential oil from a plant; it also extracted other concerns out of her mind, just as she claims her own frenzy 'banished' Malvolio's frenzy from her memory. Once married to Sebastian, her frenzy seems to pass and she can once again attend to other concerns. When Sebastian tries to figure out what is happening between him and Olivia, he is remarkably open to possibility. He knows he doesn't understand what is happening and that he is not in control of it. But he casts himself adrift on that stream anyway.

Thus Malvolio and Sebastian stand on either side of Olivia. Malvolio aspires to marry her. Olivia woos Sebastian and organizes their hasty marriage. Malvolio is treated as mad and rages against that treatment. Sebastian looks in wonder at the mad conduct he finds all around him but surrenders to it – in large part because he benefits from this madness; everything Malvolio longs for – and is ridiculed for wanting – drops into Sebastian's lap. Malvolio has another identity thrust upon him; Sebastian will answer to 'Cesario', and first introduced himself to Antonio as 'Roderigo' (2.1.16). His very identity is as fluid as the sea. Barber suggests Malvolio is also a foil for Cesario – he loves his mistress as she her master (255). Callaghan suggests he's a parallel to Orsino; they are both suitors to Olivia who can't quite see her (*Shakespeare* 37). In short, Malvolio is an outlier in some ways but a character who helps us see and understand other characters who fare better in the play.

We've been talking about history as a kind of equipment for reading the play and I've been playing the role of the more historically informed guide who conveys 'background' or 'contextual' information you might not know in order to deepen your understanding of the play. But plays teach you how to read them and this one is not an exception. In placing the play in historical context, we've considered how to group and locate the characters. We will be considering other ways in which characters are grouped and regrouped in the course of the play since reuniting separated twins and joining couples in marriage is the plot's main achievement. We've talked about topicality – how to align key characters with historical figures, types, or trends. Let me conclude this chapter by reviewing a few other ways of getting a handle on a Shakespearean play (or any complicated text), especially this one.

Opening strategies

It is often useful to identify parts of the play that for you seem to sum up its meaning or that seem particularly saturated with significance. A starting place can be **choosing one line** that, for you, captures the play's essence. For example, one might argue that Olivia's line 'I would you were as I would have you be' (3.1.140) captures all of the ways in which the characters project their desires onto others. Orsino's line 'I have unclasped / To thee the book even of my secret soul' (1.4.13–14) points to the ways in which the play is interested in people's secrets and how they do and do not open those secrets to others. Fabian's line 'If this were played upon a stage now, I could condemn it as an improbable fiction' (3.4.123–4) draws attention to the play's self-consciousness about its own status as fiction and as theatre. There are numerous other possibilities. What makes this exercise entertaining and illuminating is that there are not right or wrong answers; one's explanation for choosing a line is where the interest lies. It is also useful to think about why famous lines do not work well to sum up a play. For example, the line 'Some are born great, some achieve greatness and some have greatness thrust upon them' is particularly well known. It appears in the forged letter used to entrap Malvolio (2.5.141–3) and then is repeated (with key changes) twice more in the play. It is certainly pithy. But who is speaking here? And what are we to make of wisdom presented as bait, as what a dupe wants to hear? Look up online 'famous quotes' from the play and assess how well, for you, they sum it up. What alternatives would you propose? If there were a t-shirt for the crew of your production of *Twelfth Night*, what would you have printed on it?

You might similarly choose a **key word** or words for the play (some possibilities here are love, disguise, mad or music). A first step in selecting a word is to search a concordance, which will tell you how many times forms of that word appear in the play and how often Shakespeare used the word in other plays. See, for example, http://www.opensourceshakespeare. org/concordance/. It is also useful to identify for yourself **key scenes** in the play. We all have our own maps of a play, its peaks and valleys, the scenes and speeches we think the play could not do without and those we'd cut if we could. If you had to do a speeded up version of the play, which scenes would you focus on? And what would you call them? Critics and theatre people often come up with nicknames for scenes. The scene in which Malvolio finds the forged letter, for example, is often called 'the boxtree scene' since his tormenters hide behind the boxtree. That title places emphasis on the observers. What else might we call it? One critic, for instance, refers to it as 'the eavesdropping scene' (Ghose 115). We might also call it the 'letter scene'. Does this lead you to think differently about it? Sometimes naming a scene says something about how we interpret it. Is the first meeting between Olivia and Cesario a wooing scene? If so, who is wooing whom? What else might we call it? Is 3.4 a fight scene, a betrayal scene in which, as Antonio sees it, Sebastian refuses to acknowledge or help him, or the scene in which Viola first realizes that her brother might be alive? It is all three, of course. But what we call it shapes our understanding of its significance. Is the scene in which Malvolio is shut up in the dark and taunted as mad (4.2) the 'dark house' scene, the 'cell scene' (Berry 112), or a torture scene? Sometimes naming is even more powerful. In Act 5.2 of *Othello*, Othello says to Desdemona that her insistence on her innocence 'makes me call what I intend to do / A murder, which I thought a sacrifice' (5.2.69–70). Calling that scene a murder scene, a death scene, an assassination, or a consummation carries interpretative freight. So when a note to a play or a critical essay refers to a 'boxtree scene' or a 'wedding scene' think twice about what you would call it rather than simply adopting that terminology.

Finally, tracking **objects** can help you gain mastery over a play. Shakespeare's stage used relatively few props so those to which the texts draw our attention are often laden with meaning. In *Twelfth Night*, props include the letter Sir Toby, Maria, and the others use to 'tickle' the trout Malvolio, the letter Sir Andrew composes to challenge Cesario and that Sir Toby urges him to 'write … in a martial hand' (3.2.40), and the letter Malvolio writes to Olivia to assert his sanity and complain of his ill treatment. Malvolio begs Feste for 'a candle, and pen, ink and paper' (4.2.81) – repeating the request twice more. These letters alert us to the fact that letters are one of the most frequently called for props on the stage in the sixteenth and seventeenth centuries, both because this was a letter-writing culture and because letters do a lot of work for the plot. According to one count, letters are included in more than 400 contemporary stage directions (Dessen and Thomson 131–2). They aren't just 'props' though. Letters, like songs in the plays, seem to have circulated as separate texts, rather than forming part of the play manuscript. So an actor might hold and read the letter, rather than memorizing it. In plays, characters other than the intended recipients sometimes read letters aloud. Often, the text of a letter appears without a speech prefix to signal who reads it because it is unclear whose 'speech' a letter is. In *Twelfth Night*, is the letter Malvolio reads aloud speech we should use to evaluate Olivia (as Malvolio is led to think), Maria (who composed it) or Malvolio (who interrupts his reading of the letter to interpret it in ways that tell us a great deal about him)?

Another important object, referred to rather than seen on stage, is connected to this forged letter. Malvolio tells us that Olivia uses 'the impressure her Lucrece' (2.5.92) to seal her letters with melted wax. That is, she uses the image of Lucrece, the ancient matron who killed herself rather than live with the shame of being raped by the tyrant, Tarquin. Lucrece was a widely depicted but problematic figure for chastity. Maria uses the seal on the forged letter to reinforce its association with Olivia. In the letter Maria writes for Malvolio to find, she also writes:

> I may command where I adore,
> But silence, like a Lucrece knife,
> With bloodless stroke my heart doth gore. (2.5.103–5)

So again Maria associates Olivia with Lucrece. Through her simile, 'silence like a knife' she makes the secret of loving Malvolio parallel to the secret of rape, a secret associated with shame in the Lucrece tradition. In these two references to Lucrece, the play also draws our attention to the prospect of rape, a threat that is part of Shakespeare's source, Barnabe Riche's story of 'Apolonius and Silla', in which the Viola figure is threatened with rape and chooses to disguise herself in men's clothing in part as protection against sexual assault. In Riche's romance, the Olivia figure becomes pregnant by the Sebastian figure (Bullough). So sex outside of marriage, forced or consensual, haunts the play as a possibility. This possibility takes material form in the Lucrece seal – a seal Malvolio does not hesitate to break open, even though he cannot be sure the letter is addressed to him.

Letters and letter-writing equipment (pen, ink, paper and seal) are not the only important props in the play. Others include swords, those badges of manhood most of the men including Cesario seem to carry, and purses, the badges of economic entitlement. Olivia presses a purse on Cesario (but he spurns it) and Antonio gives his purse to Sebastian but then has to ask for it back (from Cesario). Various characters offer coins to Feste (Cesario, Sebastian, Toby and Orsino, but, interestingly, not his mistress, Olivia); Feste appears always to accept them. When Olivia tries to pay Cesario, however, he refuses. 'I am no fee'd post, lady; keep your purse' (1.5.276). In this way, he announces that he is no ordinary servant.

As coins or what we might call 'tips' were an important part of a culture of service, so gifts were crucial to courtship. Consequently, gifts circulate through this play, tracking the progress and exchange of love. The gifts include the jewel Orsino sends to Olivia (although we don't see her receive it or hear that she does [Giese 109]); the jewel Olivia gives Cesario in 3.4, which includes her picture; the pearl Olivia has given Sebastian (4.3); and the rings that the Priest claims that Olivia and Sebastian 'interchanged' to seal 'a contract of eternal bond of love' (5.1.152, 155). Olivia gives almost all the gifts in the play and, consequently, most of them go to Cesario and Sebastian. Indeed, one critic argues that in no other Shakespearean comedy 'is one character … offered so many gems'. This critic counts five, 'though Sebastian intercepts two of them' (Powers 219). What does that tell you? What can we learn about the play by tracking these objects? How can these objects help us to understand both the plot and the more abstract concerns we find registered in the play's language?

One can never account for everything in a play. But you can cultivate some strategies that will help you to achieve basic mastery of a difficult text. These strategies include grouping characters and thinking about how plot realigns them, focusing on a single character, and identifying key lines, key words, important scenes and meaningful objects. This is only the beginning of interpretation and appreciation. But it's a great start.

CHAPTER ONE

Language in print: 'tis poetical

I've suggested a variety of strategies for getting a handle on a play, including narrowing your focus to a key character, word, scene or object. The moment in the text that triggers your own interpretation can come at any time. It is as likely to appear in the middle of the play or at the end as at the beginning. Still, it is always useful to consider how a play begins and what the effects of that beginning are. Students sometimes forget how a Shakespeare play begins because Shakespeare often begins in a place very different from where the central action will be: with Iago discussing Othello and Desdemona, rather than with the couple themselves eloping; with Gloucester and his son, rather than King Lear and his daughters; with Orlando and Adam at the court rather than in the forest of Arden. Many films of the plays alter their beginnings in order to provide backstory, making it harder to remember where the playtexts start. While Shakespeare is certainly comfortable providing us with exposition – when characters hold forth about what has already happened that we need to know to understand the story that will unfold before us – he also constructs his plays carefully so that the viewer has to piece together key information as the story develops. In all of his plays, he is interested in what *Hamlet* calls 'indirection' – seeing things from a skewed perspective, hearing what people thought happened rather than seeing an important event ourselves, feeling after-shocks rather than experiencing the original impact. After you've completed reading a play, it's useful to think about where, in your understanding, the story begins and how you would compare where the story begins with where the play does. Sometimes it's useful to think about how you'd 'pitch' the story if you were trying to convince someone to make it into a movie. 'So there was a shipwreck ...'; 'So this guy is in love with this woman ...'

Shakespeare tends not to depict the beginning of the story but rather to plunge us in when the story is already underway and when one of the most exciting things to watch is how the past – what has already happened – shapes the present. That's traditionally considered the province of tragedy, in which it is impossible to shake off the constraints and consequences of what has come before. But it is true in comedy as well. Among the events that shape the characters' personalities and possibilities in *Twelfth Night* are the deaths of Olivia's father and brother and of Sebastian and Viola's father, the shipwreck, the three-month cohabitation of Antonio and Sebastian and earlier encounters between Orsino and Olivia. What else? It's also useful to think about what is part of the staged action but that Shakespeare chooses not to show: when Orsino hires Cesario, for instance. Instead of showing us that scene, Shakespeare fastforwards so that when we see Orsino and Cesario together they are already deeply attached.

The first scene

We begin with Orsino – and with music, which must be playing when the play begins, since Orsino comments on it. The play thus begins and ends with music, since it concludes with Feste's final song. The play also opens with Orsino evaluating a performance and there will be other equally self-conscious performance reviews in the course of the play (Booth 152). Lovers in Shakespearean comedy meet their matches and fall in love in the course of the plays. A character who is already in love at the start of a play is more likely to be in a tragedy than a comedy. He or she is likely to switch from one supposed love to another, or conflict or death will divide the lovers. Make of that what you will. When we meet Orsino, he is already in love, he insists, with Olivia. This suggests that Olivia is not the one he will end up with. How would you evaluate what Orsino has to say?

> If music be the food of love, play on,
> Give me excess of it, that surfeiting
> The appetite may sicken and so die.
> That strain again, it had a dying fall.
> O, it came o'er my ear like the sweet south
> That breathes upon a bank of violets,
> Stealing and giving odour. Enough, no more,
> 'Tis not so sweet now as it was before.
> O spirit of love, how quick and fresh art thou,
> That, notwithstanding thy capacity
> Receiveth as the sea, naught enters there
> Of what validity and pitch soe'er
> But falls into abatement and low price
> Even in a minute. So full of shapes is fancy
> That it alone is high fantastical. (1.1.1–15)

First, try to sum up what Orsino says here. What or who is he talking about? Then break the speech down, trying to paraphrase each sentence. That should help you capture what Orsino is saying (although be advised that this is a difficult speech. If you are not always sure, that's OK). A line of verse can be considered as a unit of thought. But that is less true in Shakespeare's plays than it is in, say, a sonnet. Here, a thought often runs across several lines of verse. Lines and sentences are not the same. When you arrive at the end of each line in this passage, has a thought been completed (usually signified by ending punctuation) or has the thought been left hanging to run over into the next line (called enjambment)? What's the effect of spillover in this passage?

Once you get a handle on what Orsino is saying, the question should become what seems noteworthy about how Orsino says it? Many students approach the challenge of 'close' or 'slow' reading of a passage by hoping and waiting for some divine inspiration. Surely if you look long enough the text will reach out and grab you, handing you the key to its mysteries. Sometimes, that happens. But more often, we have to go to the text, rather than waiting for it to come to us. The best strategy for doing so is to begin to assemble a list of questions you can ask of a passage that will help you start to break down how it works and what it means. At the end of Chapter 3 in this book, there is a summary checklist of the kinds of questions you might want to get in the habit of asking about literature.

Parts of speech

The first step to literary analysis is also an early step in language acquisition: being able to identify parts of speech and 'diagram' sentences by identifying the work each word is doing. Unfortunately, native speakers of a language often lack this ability. Attention to grammar has dropped out of the curriculum for many. But the result is an impoverished understanding of how the language we speak and read works. It may seem pointless to learn the rules with regard to Shakespeare, since he so often breaks them. Still, one needs a basic understanding of grammar to analyse a Shakespearean passage, or, indeed, any text.

A basic sentence consists of a noun – the person or thing that engages in the action, the agent or subject of the verb – and a verb, the word that conveys the action. A sentence fragment is thus a sentence that does not have those basic components and so cannot stand alone. When Sebastian agrees to be ruled by Olivia, he says 'Madam, I will' (4.1.64). While short, this is a complete sentence. I is the subject and will is the verb here. I is a pronoun, meaning that it stands in for a named noun, which is its 'antecedent'. We will focus on pronouns in the next chapter. In Orsino's first speech, we can see that attending to pronouns and their antecedents helps us pinpoint some of Orsino's vagueness. What is the 'it' in line 5? What 'falls into abatement and low price' and what do you think Orsino means by this?

There are often two nouns in a sentence, the agent or subject of the action – the doer – and the object of the action. When Viola proposes 'I'll serve this duke' (1.2.52) in her simple sentence 'I' is the subject, 'will serve' is the future tense verb, and 'this duke' is the object. But this first speech in *Twelfth Night* immediately alerts you that few sentences keep it this simple. They elaborate on the noun-verb-noun structure. But you can get a handle on more complex sentences by looking for the noun-verb-noun structure at their core. Shakespeare often inverts the word order we might expect, placing the verb at the start or the end rather than the middle, for example. When you identify complicated sentences stretching across multiple lines, pay attention to whether or how the structure emphasizes some words over others. Where are the most important words placed?

Shakespeare also complicates sentences by adding multiple clauses or subunits of meaning. Consider, for example, the long sentence in which Orsino imagines Olivia's capacity for love, given how passionately she mourns her brother.

> How will she love when the rich golden shaft
> Hath killed the flock of all affections else
> That live in her – when liver, brain and heart,
> These sovereign thrones, are all supplied, and filled
> Her sweet perfections with one self king! (1.1.34–8)

The structure of Orsino's sentence builds toward himself, the one and only king who will occupy the throne of Olivia's affections. He presents Olivia as active – she will love – but also as the victim of a violent attack from Cupid's arrow, which will kill all her other affections, and as a place or a piece of furniture, 'supplied and filled' by a new king. Two subordinate clauses (when ... when) explain the conditions that must occur before Orsino's fantasy can come true. Playing with other ways to order this complicated sentence will give you ideas about how to think about Shakespeare's choices regarding word order. One of the conventions of literary criticism is that we act as if everything is intentional, everything has a meaning, even if we can't capture an author's intention. Shakespeare hasn't left us rough drafts or a writer's notebook explaining why he did what he did. Instead, just as it is illuminating to ask how else a play might begin and why it begins as it does, so it is also useful to look at a long compli- cated sentence and consider how else it could be laid out and what the effects are of presenting it as Shakespeare does. What can you make of the fact that Orsino saves himself to the end? What do we learn about him and his love from this sentence and the conditions it sets for him to win Olivia?

Let us return to Orsino's first speech in *Twelfth Night*. In it, he introduces several nouns that will prove important in the play. These include music, appetite, love and the sea. But I want to draw your attention to another that is less familiar: fancy. The word fancy was closely connected to the word fantasy. Early modern people understood it to mean 'a creative capacity that was engaged every single time they saw, heard, smelled, tasted, and/or touched anything – or anyone, for that matter' (Bruce Smith, 'His fancy's queen' 65). It thus emphasizes the role of sense perception in stoking desire and daydreams. In addition to imagination or fantasy, it can mean variously 'delusion, whim, affectation, love-longing' (Bruce Smith 67). The word will appear often in the play. Sebastian uses it to convey his delighted surrender to Olivia's invitation: 'Let fancy still my sense in Lethe steep: / If it be thus to dream, still let me sleep' (4.1.61–2). For Sebastian, 'fancy' means an illusion, a dream he wants to keep on dreaming.

He wants that illusion to 'still' or silence his sense that this is not real. Orsino uses the word 'fancy' again to compare men and women, saying that men's 'fancies are more giddy and unfirm' than are women's (2.4.33). Here he seems to mean desires or whims. Malvolio uses the word as a verb, meaning feeling erotic desire, when he claims that Olivia told him 'that should she fancy it should be one of my complexion' (2.5.23–4). Finally, Orsino imagines a future when Cesario has changed into maiden's weeds or women's clothes and so can be seen as Viola and installed as 'Orsino's mistress and his fancy's queen' (5.1.381). As his fancy's queen, Viola will reign over his desire, capture his imagination, and occupy all of his senses. We will see other examples of words in the play that bear a range of meanings, many of which have since become obsolete, in Chapter 3.

With regard to the verbs, the first step is to identify the action words in a passage. In this passage, the verbs include be, play, give, surfeiting, sicken, die, had, came, breathes, stealing and giving, is, was, art, receiveth, enters, falls, is and is. Orsino relies heavily on versions of the verb to be (be, is, was). Among all of these verbs, which one would you select as the most important? Do you see connections among them? Note how the noun form of fall early in the passage ('dying fall') alerts us to its verb form later ('falls into abatement'). When we are thinking about action, it's also useful to think about the arc or movement in a passage. What has changed or been learned or accomplished in the course of the speech?

We will talk more about tenses later, but it is interesting here to see that while Orsino uses verbs in the present tense for the most part – describing actions that are underway – he also moves into the past tense to describe how the tune becomes less sweet than it 'was before' and he anticipates the future, a future in which his appetite sickens and dies. You might also attend to the 'voice' of verbs, that is, whether they are active or passive. Many teachers will encourage you to use active verbs in your own writing because this leads to more concise and forceful prose. You can take a first step toward more self-conscious use of active verbs in your own writing by starting to distinguish between active and passive verbs in Shakespeare's text. When Olivia concludes about Malvolio: 'He hath been most notoriously abused' (5.1.372) she uses a verb in the passive voice to explain what has been done to Malvolio rather than what he has done.

Whereas nouns, pronouns, and verbs are the basic building blocks of a sentence, sentences also often include gracenotes, the adjectives that describe a thing or person (a noun) and the adverbs that describe *how* an action is done (a verb). In this passage, 'sweet', 'quick', and 'fresh' are all adjectives. The extended simile describing the tune as like the south breeze on violets acts as a kind of adverb, describing how the tune 'came o'er' Orsino's ear. Adverbs conventionally end in '-ly'. A more familiar adverb appears in the next scene, in which Viola promises the Captain: 'I'll pay thee bounteously' (1.2.49). Bounteously is the adverb. At one level, adjectives and adverbs are unnecessary – we could grasp the sense, at the simplest level, without them. At another level, Shakespeare wouldn't be Shakespeare without these words. What do they add?

The text I've provided here is from the Arden edition of the play (as are all of the quotations in this book). You might find it useful to compare this version to others, which are readily available in books and online. But you need to know the source of those other editions. Some other volumes in this series focus on comparisons between the earliest texts of the plays. But there is only one early text of *Twelfth Night*. There are no quartos of *Twelfth Night*, that is single-play editions, because it was one of the 18 Shakespeare plays that were not published before 1623, when what has come to be called the 'First Folio' presented Shakespeare's collected works to readers. This collection appeared years after Shakespeare's death in 1616. Two actors from his company oversaw its publication. Without it, we probably would not have a record of those 18 plays that it first brought into print. Since the authoritative text of *Twelfth Night* is the First Folio, start by looking at that. You can access an online facsimile through the

Internet Shakespeare Editions website (http://internetshake-
speare.uvic.ca/Library/facsimile/). Note that to reach *Twelfth
Night* you must first go to First Folio (1623). You might
then contrast that to a readily available version such as The
Complete Works of Shakespeare (http://shakespeare.mit.edu/).
What differences do you see? Some versions, for instance, use
numerous exclamation points, making Orsino a more emphatic
and lively speaker than he appears to be here. The Folio also
places a period after 'sea' in line 11. How does that shape your
understanding of Orsino's complicated sentence? Beginning
in the eighteenth century, many editors have replaced 'sound'
with 'south' in line five. As you can see, the Arden edition does
so. Editors have a tradition of 'correcting' the plays when they
seem bewildering. Surely, it must be a breeze (from the south)
that 'breathes'! Yet substituting 'south' for 'sound' cannot
change the fact that, in this speech, Orsino mixes together
smell, taste and sound. Music *is* a food (a metaphor, equating
two apparently different things) and it is *like* the breeze (a
simile) that plays across violets, releasing their scent. This is
sometimes called synesthesia: speaking of one sense in terms
of another or associating two or more different senses in the
same image. The reference to violets might catch our attention
if our text or theatre programme advises us that we are about
to meet a character named Viola. As I've mentioned, we don't
actually hear Viola's name spoken until the end of the play.
Orsino's emphasis on music (the first noun in the play) might
also prepare us for Viola's name and her musical gifts since a
'Viol de gamba' is a musical instrument and Viola informs the
Captain that she can 'speak to him [Orsino] in many sorts of
music' (1.2.55). Note, however, that Cesario never actually
sings. If the references to music and violets might anticipate
Viola, it is striking that Orsino does not name Olivia here.
His focus is his own feelings. It was conventional for lovers to
talk about their pain and suffering. Orsino is no exception. He
claims to want to surfeit (overindulge to the point of sickness)
because his unrequited desire is so painful. But he both
seems to enjoy his torment (and has chosen an apparently

inaccessible object of desire) and to be somehow mournful.
What, precisely, does Orsino feel sad about?

Verse and prose

Orsino's opening speech is a poem. In Shakespeare's drama,
characters speak both poetry and prose. In fact, this play is
more than half prose. The division between the two roughly
follows divisions of class and genre: higher-status characters
speak in verse; lower-status characters speak in prose; tragic
heroes speak poetry, while comic characters speak prose. In
this play, for instance, the comic subplot is largely conducted
in prose. But there are telling variations. Sir Toby Belch
and Sir Andrew Aguecheek are knights who speak in prose
because they are in the comic subplot. In her first meeting
with Cesario, Olivia switches from prose to verse (at about
1.5.249): 'Your lord does know my mind: I cannot love him'.
Her shift into verse may indicate that she is falling in love and
shifting into the language that lovers speak. Cesario alternates
between verse and prose in this scene. In some ways, the
'part' Orsino has had him learn seems to be in verse, while
Cesario's attempts to actually converse with Olivia, and to
deal with the unexpected and uncooperative ways in which
she resists his performance of Orsino's love, are in prose. Yet
when Cesario goes beyond his script to say what he would
do if he loved Olivia ('Make me a willow cabin at your gate'
[1.5.260]) he does so in verse and continues to speak in verse
until he exits. He is offbook, responding to Olivia rather than
performing a memorized script, and he speaks a language that
aligns him with Olivia's high social status and strong emotion.
No wonder she is drawn to him. Malvolio's final speech
addressing Olivia is in verse, which is often the language of
sanity. In *Hamlet*, for example, Hamlet switches into prose
when he is acting mad; Ophelia degenerates from verse
into prose when she goes mad. Malvolio's use of verse thus

underscores his sanity. His use of verse also elevates his claim for sympathy. He, who aspired to marry his mistress, is finally able to speak her language at the moment he reproaches her. He, who insisted that he was not a comic butt but a victim, speaks a language of dignity and privilege, the blank verse of the tragic protagonist, when he finally escapes imprisonment and tells his side of the story.

How can we tell the difference between verse and prose? When Malvolio reads aloud the letter that Maria leaves for him to find in 2.5 of the play, he announces the shift from verse to prose in it: 'Soft, here follows prose' (2.5.138–9). How does he know? And how can we? In a printed text of a play, the layout often distinguishes verse (which is set out on the page in shorter lines) and prose (which is set in longer, enjambed lines, running margin to margin). In 2.5, for example, you can see the difference between the verse portion of the letter – 'I may command where I adore' – and the prose portion: 'If this fall into thy hand, revolve. In my stars ...'. Lines of verse will usually be the same from edition to edition. But prose will be set and lineated differently depending on edition since space rather than rhythm, rhyme or syntax dictates the length of a line. In prose, the line is over when space has run out.

Much of the verse in *Twelfth Night* is blank, that is, unrhymed iambic pentameter (or lines of ten syllables with five stresses, the stress falling on the second syllable of each foot, as in da-dum, da-dum, da-dum, da-dum, da-dum: If music be the food of love play on). Since Shakespeare doesn't invariably use rhyme, it is worth noticing when he does. Which words are connected through rhyme? What's the effect of sound repeated in a line (**alliteration** – repeating consonants; or **assonance** – repeating vowel sounds)?

When you are counting lines of verse, in order to cite them, you count a line of verse that is shared between or among speakers as one line. For example, the following is counted as one line, 1.1.16:

Curio: Will you go hunt, my lord?
Orsino: What, Curio?
Curio: The hart.

In some ways, this can seem like a technical detail, a matter of more interest to an editor than to a student. Yes, noticing this will enable you to cite the play more accurately, but that doesn't seem too exciting. What might motivate you to pay attention to this detail of layout is the fact that it alerts you to moments when several characters work together to make a line of poetry.

For example, literary critic Penny Gay draws our attention to couplets in the play – that is, two rhyming lines – and how they signal how the characters are coupling up (Gay, 'Twelfth' 437). When Olivia and Sebastian exit together at the end of 4.1, they offer a string of four rhyming couplets, one from Olivia ('Beshrew his soul for me, / He started one poor heart of mine in thee') and then two from Sebastian (stream-dream-steep-sleep) and finally one rhyming couplet they form together ('be ruled by me' ... 'O say so, and so be') (4.1.57–64). Gay also points out the many repetitions of and rhymes on love in these lines. In the next chapter, we will return to how characters conspire to create rhyming couplets in the final scene. This is a subtle but important form of connection, available for your analysis once you start to see it.

In general, paying attention to rhyme and rhythm, to the difference between poetry and prose, will open your eyes to new layers of meaning in the language. But you should also know that scanning verse – figuring out where the stresses should fall – and even distinguishing between verse and prose – can be an inexact science. Even experts sometimes disagree about how to scan a line (that is, where the stresses fall). Poets cram in extra syllables. Sometimes a rhyme seems so forced that it feels like cheating. Sometimes Shakespeare flows so rapidly between poetry and prose that it is hard to tell where one ends and the other begins.

The hunting conceit

Curio's question – 'will you go hunt?' – might seem an odd response to Orsino's opening speech. Orsino concludes on the note of loss and abstraction. Curio responds with a concrete question, a question that arrests Orsino's attention. This is the first question in a play that is filled with them. For example, Viola's first line is a question ('What country, friends, is this?' [1.21]) and she asks many of them in the course of the play. In turn, she provokes questions from others ('Whence came you, sir?' [1.5.172]). But Orsino responds to this first question not as an inquiry as to whether blood sport might perk him up but as an invitation to think about a long-standing poetic convention by which the Petrarchan lover is a hunter and the beloved he seeks is a deer or hart. 'Hart' is a homonym for 'heart'; homonyms are two words that sound the same but that have different meanings and spellings. Their similar sound provokes the listener to link them or to think about their differences. While their different spellings may now alert the reader that they are not the same word, that was not the case in Shakespeare's day. Before dictionaries standardized spelling, the same word might be spelled several different ways in a printed text (de Grazia). With the standardization of spelling, 'many words that an Elizabethan could, if he liked, spell a number of ways— 'hart'/ 'heart' is a frequent example from the courtly lyrics of the period, or 'deer'/'dear'—lose the easy intrinsic ambiguity they had previously enjoyed' (Read 86). Furthermore, since 'hart' is no longer used to describe a deer, this is a play on words that most readers will only understand if they read the gloss or note.

In most love poetry, the object of the hunt is usually the beloved. But while Curio prompts Orsino to mention Olivia for the first time, although she is presumably the cause of his melancholy in his opening speech, Orsino uses the hunting conceit to return the focus to himself. Orsino says he is already hunting the hart, 'the noblest that I have'. But why need he hunt it if he already has it?

O, when mine eyes did see Olivia first,
Methought she purged the air of pestilence;
That instant was I turned into a hart,
And my desires, like fell and cruel hounds,
E'er since pursue me. (1.1.18–22)

One of the challenges one must meet in paraphrasing Shakespeare involves re-ordering the words so that you can understand their sequence more clearly. (When I first saw Olivia, I thought she purged the air of disease. At that instant, I was turned into a stag.) Describing Olivia's effect on him, Orsino continues the synesthesia of his first speech: that is, he uses one sense to describe another, saying that seeing Olivia 'purged the air of pestilence' the way a nosegay or incense was thought to do (Dugan 242). He describes Olivia in terms of her effects on the atmosphere and on him. She is purifying or medicinal. She is also hardly present.

By referring to how the sight of her transforms him, Orsino likens himself to Acteon, a figure from classical mythology. When Acteon was out hunting, he accidentally stumbled upon the goddess Diana, spying her bathing nude. She punished him for seeing her by turning him into a stag. The hunter became the hunted and his own hounds tore him into pieces. The story of Diana and Acteon was thus a cautionary tale about the dangers of gazing upon the female beloved or of allowing one's desire to place one at the mercy of women (Vickers). In Orsino's version of the story, the sight of Olivia transforms him and his own desire for her plays the role of Acteon's hounds, pursuing him cruelly. Orsino makes the lover's pursuit of the hart a closed circuit: he is pursued by his own desire; he is pursuing himself. Where is Olivia? In Sir Philip Sidney's sixteenth-century sonnet sequence, 'Astrophil and Stella', Astrophil refers to his beloved Stella's 'absent presence'. Olivia is an 'absent presence' here as well. Perhaps it is not surprising that she proves uninterested in Orsino.

Like a cloistress: Talking about Olivia

Before we meet Olivia, we hear others talk about her. Indeed, throughout the play she remains the topic of others' conversation – from Orsino's discussion of how his love for her affects him, to Maria's channelling of her mistress's authority, to Cesario's reflections on 'What means this lady?' (2.2.17), to Malvolio's fantasies about marrying her, to Sebastian's wonder at her apparently sudden and ardent pursuit of him ('What relish is this?' [4.1.59]). In this opening scene, just as Orsino finishes talking about his desires, not for her as much as provoked by her, Valentine enters to explain that Olivia would not admit him and that her maid told him to explain to Orsino why not. One might expect that Orsino would already know this. But Valentine provides crucial background information for readers and the audience.

> The element itself till seven years' heat
> Shall not behold her face at ample view,
> But like a cloistress she will veiled walk
> And water once a day her chamber round
> With eye-offending brine – all this to season
> A brother's dead love, which she would keep fresh
> And lasting in her sad remembrance. (1.1.25–31)

Paraphrase this. What precisely has Olivia vowed here? In the next scene, the Captain further explains to Viola that 'They say' that Olivia 'hath abjured the company / And sight of men' (1.2.37–8) in response to her brother's death. His source of information is, then, gossip, what others say about Olivia. Valentine links Olivia's tears to the sea from which Viola emerges in the next scene, the sea in which she thinks she has lost her brother. Olivia will water her chamber with salt water, brine, or tears to 'season' her brother's love (the way one might preserve or 'cure' meats with salt) and to 'keep' his love – both hers for him and his for her – 'fresh and lasting in her sad remembrance'(1.1.29–31). As presented by Valentine, Olivia's vow seeks to manage her grief and to perpetuate it; to honour her brother and to resist the passage of time. We've talked about word order. Notice the placement of 'dead' in the phrase 'a brother's dead love'. Does it modify brother or love? In Modern English, we prefer word order that expresses the direct relationship between modifier or adjective and noun. Shakespeare is not bound by this convention. For example, in the final scene, Cesario refers to 'my masculine usurped attire' (5.1.246), where in Modern English we would be more likely to refer to 'usurped masculine attire' (Blake, *Shakespeare's Language* 69). Based on this opening scene, we might surmise that what links Orsino and Olivia is an emphasis on loss and emotion. Orsino objects to Olivia's vow because it is 'but to a brother' (1.1.33), thus downplaying familial or sibling attachments, and because it removes Olivia from his reach. But perhaps this is also what makes him so interested in her.

Embedded in Valentine's announcement of Olivia's vow is some criticism of its content. In England after the Reformation, Valentine's decision to liken Olivia to a 'cloistress' – that is, not only a nun but a nun in an enclosed or cloistered order, with minimal contact with the outside world – might cast suspicion upon her vow, at least for some members of the audience. After the Reformation in England, there were no longer convents (or monasteries) in England. Women who wished to become nuns had to leave England to join convents in Catholic countries (breaking the law to do so). Some historians point out that the closing of convents meant the loss for some women of a viable alternative to marriage. So, from one perspective, to act 'like a cloistress' was to be marked as dated or odd. The drive to 'reform' Catholicism that led to the Reformation and the break of the Church of England from the Church of Rome was driven, in part, by suspicion of clerical celibacy as unnatural, unnecessary and hypocritical and by a defence of marriage as equal to virginity as a way of life. From this point of view, turning one's house into a kind of nunnery and withdrawing from any contact with men and air is excessive and unsustainable. However, if one is sympathetic rather than hostile to Catholicism, or interested in alternatives to marriage for women and in women's autonomy, one might view Olivia's vow positively. Is it foolish or admirable for a woman to take the veil, a common expression for taking one's vows as a nun, and cloister herself?

The message for women after the Reformation was mixed. While choosing a life of clerical celibacy and enclosure in a cloister was often disparaged as a silly waste, it was still the case that the virtuous woman was advised to shield herself from seeing or being seen. As Richard Brathwaite, for instance, wrote in his conduct manual for English gentlewomen:

> What an excellent impregnable fortress were *Woman*, did not her *Windows* betray her to her enemy? But principally, when she leaves her Chamber to walk on the public Theatre; when she throws off her veil, and gives attention to a merry tale; when she consorts with youthful blood, and either enters parley, or admits of an interview with love. It is most true what the sententious moral sometimes observed: We may be in *security*, so long as we are sequestered from *society*. Then, and never till then, begins the *infection* to be dispersed, when the sound and sick begin to be promiscuously mixed. Tempt not Chastity; hazard not your Christian liberty. (Brathwaite 43)

Brathwaite's advice is excessive, depicting any venturing out of one's house, looking out windows or lifting one's veil, as exposing one's self to infection, mixing promiscuously with the sick. The only way to remain safe is to be sequestered from society, locked away. Yet the cloister, the extreme manifestation of this practise of virtue, was denigrated. Furthermore, the virtuous woman was still expected to marry (even if not all women did).

Olivia's vow serves the plot. It is the reason Viola cannot try to get a job in her household and must instead dress as a man to work for Orsino as well as the reason that Orsino needs a messenger to carry his suit to Olivia. But it is easy for readers and viewers of the play to forget this vow because Olivia so quickly sets it aside upon meeting Cesario. Whereas Olivia at first wears a veil to signal her mourning and to shield herself from Orsino's ambassador, she also lifts that veil at Cesario's request, granting him face-to-face access to her, which Orsino never achieves until the final scene. When she lifts her veil, she 'enters parley, or admits of an interview with love'. According to Brathwaite, she thereby risks contamination. In the play, she enters the comic process of falling in love and finding a mate; she resumes a life interrupted by grief.

Just as the play's plot works against Olivia's vow, so other characters argue against it. Feste exposes the illogic of Olivia's mourning – if her brother is in heaven then why does she grieve? In Viola, we have a foil to Olivia. Many students use the word 'foil' without thinking about what it means. 'Foil' first referred to a thin sheet of metal placed under or behind a precious stone to enhance its luster and make it sparkle more brightly. By extension, it came to mean, according to the *Oxford English Dictionary* (*OED*), 'Anything that serves by contrast of color or quality to adorn another thing or set it off to advantage'. With this meaning, it is used more specifically to describe how one character in literature relates to another. Thinking about the word's etymology helps us to understand that a foil is a revealing contrast not a mirror image. In this case, it is useful to contrast Viola as a foil to Olivia. Viola, too, has lost a beloved brother. Her third line in the play is 'My brother he is in Elysium' (1.2.3). But she chooses not to enclose herself for seven years. Quite the opposite. She finds a job in a household of men; she takes a man's role. As Cesario, Viola argues that it is wrong for Olivia to remove herself from love and reproduction. Cesario says to Olivia: 'you do usurp yourself for what is yours to bestow is not yours to reserve' (1.5.182–3). Why not? 'Lady, you are the cruell'st she alive/ If you will lead these graces to the grave/ And leave the world no copy' (1.5.233–5). Cesario here voices the view that one is obligated to engage in sexual reproduction; to withhold one's self from it is ungenerous and unnatural. Both Olivia and Viola will ultimately follow the basic comic logic that one must be more attached to the living than to the dead.

Valentine's speech offers us crucial explication for the status quo at the beginning of the play: Olivia's refusal to receive Orsino's suit. But it is also an opportunity to see how a single word – here 'cloistress' – can open up an historical range of meaning and a reminder that while we need to collect evidence of how characters evaluate one another within a play world we need not share their judgements. The fact that characters in the play articulate a view doesn't mean that the play or playwright necessarily endorses it or that we need to accept it as true. Here at the start of the play, we can get in the habit of grasping the difference between making a generalization about how the world works and making and supporting an argument about how the play *presents it as* working. Cesario argues that Olivia's vow is a foolish one – but that's because it is the obstacle to his suit on Orsino's behalf. The plot leads Olivia to break her vow – but that's because this is a romantic comedy with an urgent drive toward marriage and reproduction. While textual evidence enables us to say that the play presents marriage as the happy ending for all three of its female characters, the evidence does not support the claim that this is the way it was in the early modern period or the way it is now, the truth of human experience. Can you see the difference between a textually supportable claim and a vague generalization? Between an argument and an assertion?

Carpe diem

Just as Orsino's opening speech engages the hunting conceit common in love poetry at the time, the play also self-consciously links itself to two other traditions of love poetry. One is the 'carpe diem' tradition. Carpe diem is a Latin command to 'seize the day', or, more generally, seize upon fleeting opportunity. In carpe diem poems, a speaker, usually male, urges an addressee, usually female, to seize and enjoy her youth – by having sex with him. In this tradition, the speaker and suitor takes 'no' to him as 'no' to sex and 'no' to life itself. In comic logic, as in the carpe diem poem, to say no, to withhold one's self from sexual circulation, is to refuse life and waste youth. When Cesario says to Olivia – 'you do usurp yourself for what is yours to bestow is not yours to reserve' (1.5.182–3) – he speaks within this tradition. The flower is a key image in the carpe diem tradition. For example, in Robert Herrick's poem 'Gather Ye Rosebuds' the rosebud figures the young body and the urgent passage of time. If one doesn't gather the roses while they are in bud, then they will bloom and blast and the opportunity will be past. As Feste puts it in a song, 'Youth's a stuff will not endure' (2.3.51). The insistence on time's urgent passage, on the loss of youth and what Orsino describes as the sickening and dying of the satisfied appetite, can become a kind of threat. Since time will not allow anyone to possess and control the body anyway, the speaker argues that his addressee should submit to his demand – and quickly.

Twelfth Night captures the combination of threat, sorrow and longing in carpe diem poetry in an exchange between Cesario and Orsino. In response to Cesario's confession that the one he loves is of Orsino's own age, Orsino objects that such a woman would be too old.

> Let still the woman take
> An elder than herself; so wears she to him,
> So sways she level in her husband's heart.
> For, boy, however we do praise ourselves,
> Our fancies are more giddy and unfirm,
> More longing wavering, sooner lost and worn
> Than women's are. (2.4.29–35)

Orsino goes on to make the connection between women and flowers explicit:

For women are as roses, whose fair flower
Being once displayed doth fall that very hour.

Cesario agrees:

And so they are. Alas that they are so,
To die even when they to perfection grow. (2.4.38–41)

As we will discuss in the next chapter, Cesario's use of
pronouns is almost always telling. How does the third person
plural pronoun operate here?

Blazon

Another way that the play links itself to the assumptions and
conventions of love poetry is through the blazon. In poetry, this
means a poem that breaks the beloved's attributes down into
a list, praising her as a set of features, features often described
in terms of the objects (flowers, jewels) they resemble. In
an influential argument about the fourteenth-century Italian
poet Petrarch, an important influence on English Renaissance
poetry, Nancy Vickers argues that the speaker of Petrarch's
sonnets always describes his beloved, Laura, 'as a part or parts
of a woman. When more than one part figures in a single poem,
a sequential, inclusive ordering is never stressed. Her textures
are those of metals and stones; her image is that of a collection
of exquisitely beautiful disassociated objects' (Vickers 96).
While some critics have argued that this descriptive strategy
allows the male speaker to divide and conquer, reducing the
beloved to fragments and mastering them within the bounds
of his verse, others have argued that the scattering also serves
to distribute attention across the body, rather than focusing
on the genitals, and can be viewed as an erotic celebration
of the female body's value and beauty (Parker, *Literary* 131;
Montrose 325; Traub, *Renaissance* 145).

There are many examples of blazons in sixteenth- and seventeenth-century poetry. In Edmund Spenser's sonnet sequence *Amoretti*, for example, sonnet 64 describes the beloved as smelling like gillyflowers or carnations and her cheeks as resembling or smelling like red roses, her bosom like a strawberry bed, etc. These detailed catalogues became so conventional that they generated satires, such as a picture of a monstrous woman making the similes literal, with eyes like the sun and roses on her cheeks. In Shakespeare's own sonnet 130, he defies these conventions, having the speaker insist that his mistress's eyes are *nothing* like the sun.

> My mistress' eyes are nothing like the sun;
> Coral is far more red than her lips' red.
> If snow be white, why then her breasts are dun;
> If hairs be wires, black wires grow on her head.
> I have seen roses damasked, red and white,
> But no such roses see I in her cheeks;
> And in some perfumes is there more delight
> Than in the breath that from my mistress reeks.
> I love to hear her speak, yet well I know
> That music hath a far more pleasing sound.
> I grant I never saw a goddess go:
> My mistress when she walks treads on the ground.
> And yet, by heaven, I think my love as rare
> As any she belied with false compare.

Although the speaker describes realistic features including 'reeking' breath, he also praises his mistress as walking on the ground rather than as a goddess on a pedestal and avers that she is more lovely than those women other poets praise in exaggerated or hyperbolic terms. Some students misread Shakespeare's 'anti-blazon' sonnet as critical of the mistress herself. The poem makes it clear that the target of its satire is other poets' 'false compare' of their mistresses, a strategy of comparison that 'belies' or obscures women's real attributes. When *Twelfth Night* refers to and employs the blazon, then, it draws on a familiar, widely used poetic convention.

The word 'blazon' originally means, as a noun, a shield used in battle, a coat of arms, or a banner bearing one's coat of arms. The *Oxford English Dictionary* lists the appearance of the word in *Twelfth Night* 1.5, to which we will return below, as an example of this meaning. It could also mean, as an extension of these meanings, a description or record of any kind, especially a record of virtues or positive attributes. The word can also be used as a verb, meaning not the record of praise but the process of praising: to paint, describe, to adorn; to describe appropriately and positively; to boast of. As Patricia Parker explains, the blazon had both a 'static sense' – meaning either 'the heraldic shield which stood as a sign of a particular family, name, and property', or the list of the beloved woman's attributes – 'and a more active or kinetic one: the "proclamation" or "publishing"' of this description to a wider audience (Parker, *Literary* 127). So the word 'blazon' brings together both the gazed upon and beloved object and the process of unfolding it to others' view. The blazon also introduces a third party, then, the person to whom the speaker displays the beauty of his beloved.

How is the blazon relevant to this play? Its importance becomes clear in 1.5, when Cesario woos Olivia. We have built up toward this meeting in the preceding scenes, meeting Orsino, hearing Orsino (1.1 and 1.4) and Maria, Sir Toby, and Sir Andrew (1.3) discuss Olivia, meeting Viola and then Cesario, and hearing the brief Orsino gives Cesario as his proxy suitor. Here at last we meet Olivia and, like Cesario, we must cope with her choice to withhold a view of herself, at least at first. When Cesario complains about her veil, Olivia says:

> I will give out divers schedules of my beauty. It shall be inventoried, and every particle and utensil labeled to my will: as, item, two lips, indifferent red; item, two gray eyes, with lids to them; item, one neck, one chin, and so forth. (1.5.236–40)

Olivia's reference to her will evokes both the idea of dictating a will by which she bequeaths her property to others after her death and her volition, as in the subtitle 'or what you will', by which she labels her own attributes as she wills. This mocking inventory invokes both business – the inventory of the merchandise she has to offer – and death. It suggests both that she asserts ownership of herself and that she is marketing or distributing her assets to others. After performing a kind of blazon of her own attributes, Olivia makes explicit reference to the 'blazon' when she says of Cesario: 'Thy tongue, thy face, thy limbs, actions and spirit / Do give thee fivefold blazon' (1.5.284–5). Here she refers to how Cesario's speech, appearance and bearing prove that he is, as he claims to be, a gentleman. So Olivia both performs a blazon – listing Cesario's features – and argues that these features themselves display or trumpet (blazon) Cesario's gentle birth. This reminds us of the heraldic meaning of the blazon, indicating one's heritage.

As we have seen, many critics describe the blazon as a strategy by which the male lover/speaker asserts mastery over his beloved. Olivia explains the need for such mastery when she describes how the very attributes or perfections of Cesario, the object of her desire, have invaded her: 'Methinks I feel this youth's perfections / With an invisible and subtle stealth / To creep in at mine eyes' (1.5.288–90). Cesario, then, both provokes and inspires blazons from Olivia. Like the beloved lady of sonnets, Cesario is an invention, the remote, fictional beloved. But notice, too, that Maria blazons Malvolio in her letter: 'wherein by the colour of his beard, the shape of his leg, the manner of his gait, the expressure of his eye, forehead, and complexion, he shall find himself most feelingly personated' (2.3.151–4). She mirrors his own fantasy of himself as desired and loved by Olivia. Recognizing his own fantasy in her description, Malvolio falls vulnerable to her 'device'. As one critic puts it, 'yet just as he feels he finds himself, Malvolio loses himself' (Davis 202). He, in turn, finds on the envelope containing the letter a reduction of Olivia to a body part, a crude parody of the blazon, to which we will return below in Chapter 3.

In short, comparing these moments of the play to the poetic convention of the blazon helps us notice them and their relations to one another. It is too easy to dismiss something as 'merely conventional', especially when the convention in question is not one that is still conventional in our own speech. Conventions often command our attention precisely because they are conventional, that is, so integrated into ways of thinking about and describing the world that they can disappear into invisibility. Why keep repeating a turn of phrase or writing in a form that has become conventional? What makes a particular convention useful? Recognizing the poetic convention of the blazon in *Twelfth Night* helps us see an interesting twist. If the blazon is a convention for describing the usually female beloved, it becomes noteworthy that, in *Twelfth Night*, Olivia blazons herself and female characters, Olivia and Maria, perform blazons of male characters, Cesario (in earnest) and Malvolio (in satire). In both cases, the female speaker has the upperhand. As a poetic convention as much about social power as it is about desire, the blazon may help to give them that advantage.

In this chapter, we've begun to think about the play's poetry, reading Orsino's opening speech and placing pressure on the hunting conceit, his description of himself as Acteon and Valentine's report of Olivia's vow to cloister herself. We have considered the appearance of the carpe diem convention and blazon in this play. How do you turn this kind of careful reading into your own writing?

Writing matters

Think about organization

As we've discussed, beginnings aren't inevitable. Many productions and films begin not with Orsino but with the shipwreck or Viola's washing ashore in scene two. This convention of re-ordering the play's first scenes began with a theatrical practicality. In the eighteenth and nineteenth centuries, as sets became more elaborate, it was more efficient to give audiences a quick sense of the seaside before moving to the play's two main locations, Orsino's and Olivia's houses (Osborne, *Trick* 47–8). This re-ordering also accommodated the sense that the shipwreck that brings the twins to Illyria's shore is the crucial event that sets the story moving. But directors have not stopped with this rearrangement. The play depends on two-person scenes, one-on-one intimate exchanges between two speakers, usually involving one of the twins (1.2, 2.1, 2.2, 3.3, etc.). These scenes were often reordered, especially in the nineteenth century. For example, in the Folio text of the play, Sebastian first appears in between the scene in which Olivia realizes she has fallen for Cesario and sends Malvolio after him with the ring (1.5) and the scene in which Malvolio approaches Cesario with the ring (2.2). But many nineteenth-century performances rearrange these scenes so that Sebastian does not appear until after Cesario has acknowledged that Olivia loves him: 'She loves me sure' (2.2.22). This rearrangement positions Sebastian as the solution to the 'problem' of 'poor' Olivia's love for Cesario, the means of untying the hard knot Cesario cannot (Osborne, *Trick* 48–9). The unfolding of Orsino's relationship to Cesario has also been rearranged. In Trevor Nunn's 1996 film, he 'disperses brief sections of the two early private conversations between Orsino and Cesario, in act 1 scene 4 and act 2 scene 4, so that Cesario, in effect, interacts with Orsino throughout the film and within numerous intimate settings' (Osborne, 'Marriage' 102). Keir Elam, the editor of the Arden edition, argues that the 'restless rearrangement' made in productions of the play suggests that 'the structure of the play ... is modular rather than linear' (Elam intro 97). That is, it consists of units that can be re-ordered. Propose cuts and reordering for performance and make your case for why they are necessary. Or argue for why the play needs to begin with Orsino.

Focus on a word

In order to think more deeply about a given word, your best strategy is to begin with the *Oxford English Dictionary*, but this is a resource that is available only by subscription. If you have access to a library that subscribes to the *OED*, after you search for your chosen term, you should come to a page that asks you to choose the sense of the word you are looking for. For example, the word 'blazon' can be used as either a noun or a verb; you can select *blazon, n.* (noun) or *blazon, v.* (verb) (there may be multiple choices here – v.2, n.2). Other common choices on this page are 'a.' (adjective) and 'adv.' (adverb). If there is only one set of meanings for a word, you will be taken directly to a page describing the word. There will be a list of several definitions of the word.

You will want to look at the 'full entry' for your word. For help, click on the 'help' button at the top of the screen or click on 'how to use the *OED*' on the home page. If you need definitions of the abbreviations commonly used in the *OED*, you can find these under 'how to use the *OED*'. For 'blazon', if you select *blazon, n*, you will be given five definitions beginning with 'A shield used in war'. This definition is followed by *Obs.*, which means obsolete. In other words, the word is no longer used in that sense. The obsolete meanings are often significant when we are analysing Shakespeare's works. Each entry is followed by several dated quotations, indicating instances of the word's use with this particular definition. Under the second meaning for blazon as a noun, 'A shield in heraldry; armorial bearings, coat of arms; a banner bearing the arms', for example, you will find a line from *Twelfth Night*: 'Thy tongue, thy face, thy limbes, actions, and spirit, Do giue thee fiue-fold blazon'. The *OED* suggests that the word was first used with this meaning in 1325 and lists as its last example the quotation from *Twelfth Night*. The *OED* is not always correct. Our ever-expanding ability to digitize and search texts is greatly expanding our knowledge of word uses. But the *OED* is a good place to start. I also recommend *Shakespeare's Words* (http://www.shakespeareswords.com) both because it focuses on Shakespeare and because it is open access so anyone can use it from any computer. If you type in 'blazon' in the search box on this website, you will find the seven times Shakespeare uses the word, as well as a glossary giving four meanings for it. If you click on a meaning, it will show you where Shakespeare uses the word with that particular meaning. *Shakespeare's Words* will tell you less about the word's derivation, history, and range of use than will the *Oxford English Dictionary*. But combining a Shakespeare concordance and a glossary, this website gives you a quick snapshot of a word's meaning and how Shakespeare uses it.

Another of the words we discussed in this chapter, 'cloistress', appears as the only example in the *OED* of an obsolete and rare word for 'A female tenant of a cloister, a nun', created by adding the feminine suffix -ess to the more common noun 'cloisterer' for 'one who dwells in a cloister; a monk or nun'. Be prepared for discoveries like this. Shakespeare invented lots of new words. Similarly, the use of 'extracting' to mean distracting in Olivia's description of 'a certain extracting frenzy of mine own' that banished Malvolio's distress from her memory appears only once in Shakespeare; what's more, the *OED* lists its appearance in *Twelfth Night* as the only instance in which the word was used in this way. Yet another rare word is 'sneck' which Shakespeare again uses only once, as an insult Sir Toby levels at Malvolio: 'Sneck up!' (2.3.91–2). The *Shakespeare's Words* website does not include 'sneck' in its glossary. The Arden editor suggests it means 'go hang yourself'. One can get to this meaning in the *OED* by looking up 'snick' rather than sneck. It gives the *Twelfth Night* instance as an example. But if we look up 'sneck' rather than 'snick' in the *OED* we find that 'sneck up' means shut up because of its meaning to shut and lock a gate or door by means of a sneck or latch. Isn't it most likely that Sir Toby means 'shut up?' since what he wants, above all, is for Malvolio to stop talking? This example suggests the value of approaching your edition's glosses critically rather than simply accepting them on faith; of using several reference works; and of thinking creatively about how you go about searching. If the text says 'sneck' why not look up 'sneck'?

Shakespeare is credited with using 1,700 words for the first time, including compounds (bloodstained, watchdog), some of which became standard English (obscene, excellent, frugal, majestic) and some of which did not (including cloistress, superdainty and anthropophaginian, a word for a cannibal from *The Merry Wives of Windsor*). He also routinely repurposed words, such as using gossip as a verb for the first time, or using extracting to mean distracting with the added connotation of removed from one's self. About half of the words for which Shakespeare appears to have been the first user are still in use (Crystal).

If you are writing a paper on a single word, you should also try looking it up in a Shakespeare Concordance such as http://www.opensourceshakespeare.org/concordance/. A concordance enables you to see how often a given word appears in the play and where else it appears in Shakespeare's works. This enables you to identify a unique occurrence of a term (such as cloistress) or a word Shakespeare uses often (such as mad). According to the open source concordance, Shakespeare uses 'mad' 247 times, but it appears most often in *Twelfth Night*. 'Madness' appears 68 times, most in *Hamlet* (18) but with *Twelfth Night* a distant second (five).

The limits of paraphrase

We've seen that paraphrase is an important first step in grasping the meaning of a difficult passage. Letting someone else do the paraphrasing for you will usually limit its usefulness. This is especially true with study guides and websites that include errors. But even when a paraphrase is accurate, it strips out all of the complexities and gracenotes of expression that distinguish Shakespeare. Let's face it. He borrowed his plots.

What distinguishes him is how he tells a story and how his characters express themselves. As one critic I know puts it, 'Shakespeare in other words isn't Shakespeare'. To probe the limits of paraphrase and plot summary, examine online resources and study guides for mistakes and omissions. What wouldn't you know if you only used these resources? What do we miss if we let someone other than Shakespeare tell us the story? Another possible approach to this question would be writing a treatment for a 'Shakespeare Re-told' version of *Twelfth Night* and then critiquing the proposal in terms of its neglect of the play's linguistic riches and pleasures.

Analyse a particular passage

Follow the method we used above with regard to Orsino's first speech but choose another speech. Consider some of the following rhetorical devices as well. The point is not to list everything you can think of. It is, rather, to start with this approach and then to decide which devices, of all you've noticed, will most reward extended attention.

Tropes

Figures of speech are often called 'tropes', from a word that means turning because they sometimes turn, twist or transfer a word or phrase to make it mean something new or different. The play itself is very self-conscious about its use of tropes. For example, the following exchange between Feste and Cesario draws our attention to the role of 'turning' in a literary trope.

> FESTE: To see this age! A sentence is but a cheverel glove to a good wit: how quickly the wrong side may be turned outward.
> VIOLA: Nay, that's certain. They that dally nicely with words may quickly make them wanton.

FESTE: I would, therefore, my sister had had no name, sir.
VIOLA: Why, man?
FESTE: Why, sir, her name's a word, and to dally with
that word might make my sister wanton. But indeed
words are very rascals since bonds disgraced them.
(3.1.11–20)

In this exchange, a clever person who knows how to dally
with words can turn a sentence inside out like a goatskin (or
cheverel) glove. But as the end of the exchange suggests, this
wordplay is gendered. To dally with his sister's name is to
make her 'wanton', to damage her sexual reputation. In this
exchange, words and word order are flexible, reversible. But
they are also powerful – they can make a sister wanton. It
might be argued that the plot of *Twelfth Night* replays 'the
activity of tropes' by tracking how Viola turns from female
clothes to men's, and Sebastian and Cesario change places as
Olivia's husband (Parker, *Literary* 39).

Tropes of repetition

Twelfth Night is particularly rich in rhetorical figures that
involve repetition or doubling. In each instance, these forms of
repetition help us to notice how two words are both the same
and different, like the twins, Viola and Sebastian. Tropes are
often used to describe things that can be difficult to explain
(such as love) and in their indirection they concede that they
cannot fully capture the essence of the object described.
Similarly, Viola and Sebastian may be mirror images of one
another, they may be interchangeable in some ways, but, in the
end, they cannot substitute for one another. Like homonyms,
Cesario and Sebastian look or sound the same but are different.
The repetition in *Twelfth Night* often emphasizes how doubles
or mirrors create confusion or multiply meanings. Double also
has the connotation not just of multiplication but of deception
or 'double dealing' (Parker, *Literary* 74–5). Here are some

crucial figures that depend on doubles and mirror images, as well as examples of their appearance in the play.

Anadiplosis: One line begins with the same word or phrase with which the last one ended. The term comes from the Greek for doubling back (Wales 276–7). If a single speaker uses this figure it can convey a sense of building urgency. In an exchange in which one speaker echoes the other, the repetition can convey either intimacy or misunderstanding. Consider the following:

> MALVOLIO: 'Remember who commended thy yellow
>   stockings' –
> OLIVIA: Thy yellow stockings?
> MALVOLIO: 'And wished to see thee cross-gartered'.
> OLIVIA: Cross gartered? (3.4.45–9)

Normally we would expect this echoing to indicate listening closely. But in this extended exchange, Malvolio thinks he is quoting from Olivia's own letter, so that she will immediately recognize his mandate to behave as he has. Olivia has no idea what he is talking about and his quotations just alienate and confuse her further.

Anaphora: Repetition of the same word(s) at the beginning of successive lines or clauses. Many of the characters in the play use this figure. Malvolio explains to Olivia how he tried to get rid of Cesario: '*I told him you were* sick ... *I told him you were* asleep' (1.5.136–8). When he imagines his new life as Olivia's beloved he vows: '*I will* be proud, *I will* read politic authors, *I will* baffle Sir Toby, *I will* wash off gross acquaintance, *I will* be point-device the very man' (2.5.157–9). Olivia tries to make short work of Cesario by saying '*if you* be not mad, be gone. / *If you* have reason, be brief' (1.5.194–5). In this same scene, she proposes to create an inventory of her attributes: '*item, two* lips, indifferent red; *item, two* grey eyes, with lids to them' (1.5.239–40). Cesario claims that Orsino loves Olivia '*with* adoration's fertile tears, / *With* groans that thunder love, *with* sighs of fire' (1.5.247–8) (this is hyperbole as well, as so many descriptions of Orsino's feelings are). He later claims to love Orsino 'More than I love these eyes, *more* than my life, / More by all mores than e'er I shall love wife' (5.1.131–2). In the final scene, Sebastian begs Cesario for information: 'Of charity, *what* kin are you to me? / *What* countryman? *What* name? *What* parentage?' (5.1.226–7). In all of these examples, the repetition adds emphasis. (Many of these examples could also be connected to *Isocolon* – phrases of equal length and comparable structure.)

Antanaclasis: Repeating the same word with a different sense. In *Twelfth Night*, Feste puts on a clergyman's gown and remarks: 'I will *dissemble* myself in't and I would I were the first that ever *dissembled* in such a gown' (4.2.4–6). Feste shifts the meaning of *dissemble* from 'disguise' to 'act hypocritically' (Keller). Responding to Sir Toby's claim that Andrew has 'all the good *gifts* of nature', Maria says that Sir Andrew has 'The *gift* of a coward' which may well land him 'the *gift* of a grave' (1.3.25–6, 29, 31). She thus shifts the meaning of 'gift' from a talent or aptitude to a present. At the end of the play, Feste and Olivia play with the word 'delivered'. Feste says 'but, as a madman's epistles are no gospels so it skills not much when they are *delivered*... . Look then to be well edified, when the fool *delivers* the madman' (5.1.283–7). Olivia replies 'See him *delivered*' (5.1.309). In the course of this exchange, deliver has three meanings: give to (as in delivering the mail), speak the words of (as in delivering a speech someone else has written) and release (as in deliver from bondage).

Another example of antanaclasis would be the multiple meanings of 'cut' in 1.3, discussed below.

Asteismus: Responding to someone else by exploiting the multiple meanings of his or her own words. Since asteismus requires a speaker to work with what he or she has been given, picking up a word from another speaker and twisting its meaning, it requires close attention to an interlocutor's words and turns of phrase. When Cesario inquires as to whether Olivia is 'the lady of the house' in 1.5, Olivia responds 'If I do not *usurp* myself, I am' and Cesario shifts the meaning of the word 'usurp', saying 'Most certain if you are she you do *usurp* yourself, for what is yours to bestow is not yours to reserve' (1.5.179–83). The tables can also be turned on Cesario as in this exchange with Feste:

> VIOLA: Dost thou *live by* thy tabor?
> FESTE: No sir, I *live by* the church. (3.1.1–2).

Here the play is on the phrase 'live by', meaning both 'make your living by means of' and 'dwelling nearby'. I've mentioned the similarities between Feste and Cesario. It is interesting to see that they share a gift for asteismus, or appropriating and twisting another's words. In another example, Malvolio asks Sir Toby 'Is there no respect of place, persons, nor *time* in you?' and Sir Toby responds, 'We did keep *time*, sir, in our catches' (2.3.89–91), shifting from Malvolio's meaning of time ('time of day') to the musical meaning of keeping a steady pace and coordinating with other singers or players. Asteismus is a particularly revealing instance of a pattern by which 'when characters repeat words and sentences in *Twelfth Night*, they either misunderstand them or give them a new meaning unintended by the original speaker' (Keller 147).

Chiasmus (sometimes called *antimetabole*): Certain words, sounds, concepts or sentence structures are repeated in reverse order. The term is derived from the Greek letter chi, which is x-shaped – the two parts of the chiastic device mirror each other, as do the parts of the letter x.

When Olivia reprimands Feste that he is a dry fool and grows dishonest, he responds:

> Two faults, madonna, that drink and good counsel will amend: for give the *dry fool* drink, then is the *fool* not *dry*; bid the *dishonest* man *mend* himself – if he *mend*, he is no longer *dishonest*, if he cannot, let the botcher *mend* him. Anything that's *mend*ed is but *patched*: *virtue* that trangresses is but *patched* with *sin*, and *sin* that amends is but *patched* with *virtue*. (Feste 1.5. 39–45)

Ploce: Repetition of the same word, sometimes after the intervention of one or two other words. For example, Malvolio accuses Olivia: 'Madam, you have done me *wrong*, / Notorious *wrong*' (5.1.322–3). Repeating the word 'wrong' with the intensifying adjective 'notorious', Malvolio emphasizes the gravity of the offence against him. Cesario tells Olivia that he loves Orsino '*More* than I love these eyes, *more* than my life, / *More* by all *mores* than e'er I shall love wife' (5.1.131–2). Cesario uses 'more' here as an adverb, describing how he loves Orsino, but also plays with it as a noun, 'more by all mores', as if mores are a category of things. In a final example, Feste quips 'Nothing that is so is so' (4.1.8), depending on the echo of 'is so' not to intensify, as repetitions often do, as in the preceding two examples, but to undo or reverse.

Polyptoton: Repeating the same word in different forms, perhaps with the addition or subtraction of prefixes or suffixes. We see this when Maria advises Sir Toby that 'Your cousin, my lady, takes great *exceptions* to your ill hours' and he responds by playing on the word exception and asserting his own capacity to take exception to her taking exception: 'Why, let her *except*, before *excepted*' (1.3.4–6). Olivia remarks to Cesario that 'Love *sought* is good, but given *unsought* is better' (3.1.154). The most famous instance of polyptoton in the play is probably the line 'Some are born *great*, some achieve *greatness* and some have *greatness* thrust upon them' (2.5.141–3), which is also an example of anaphora. Malvolio later quotes these lines again (3.4) and Feste quotes them in the last scene. Interestingly, in this instance of repetition, Feste misremembers the lines. He says 'Some are born great, some achieve greatness and some have greatness thrown [rather than thrust] upon them' (5.1.364–5). He also misremembers Malvolio's line to Olivia 'Unless you laugh and minister occasion to him, he is gagged' as 'an you smile not, he's gagged' (1.5.82–3; 5.1.369). On the one hand, this is realistic. Feste remembers the force of the insult rather than the exact wording. On the other hand, in a play about both mirror images and misrecognition, he holds up a slightly distorted mirror of what the letter said and what Malvolio said.

Syllepsis: A word with two or more meanings, more usually called a pun. (By the way, 'pun' is a word that entered the English language only after Shakespeare's death. We now use 'pun' as a verb [to pun on] or noun [a pun] to describe exploiting a word's multiple meanings and so alerting the reader or listener to those meanings.) When Cesario says, probably in an aside, that 'A little thing would make me tell them how much I lack of a man' (3.4.290), he uses the phrase 'little thing' to mean both that the slightest provocation would get him to admit that he is a coward and that what he lacks is the 'little thing' or penis that would make him a man. Many of the examples above of asteismus depend on this kind of punning, picking up a word used with one meaning and deliberately misunderstanding it as having another meaning.

Although I would argue that these figures that double, twin, or mirror words are particularly important in the play, they are not, of course, the only ones that matter. Among **other figures that are important in the play** are the following.

Antithesis: The grammatically parallel presentation of opposing ideas. The classic example of antithesis is the first line of Charles Dickens's novel *A Tale of Two Cities*: 'It was the best of times, it was the worst of times ...' *Twelfth Night* is also structured around comparisons and oppositions. These inform the play's language in antithetical statements such as Cesario's claim that 'I am one that had rather go with Sir Priest than Sir Knight' (3.4.264–5), meaning that he would prefer not to fight Sir Andrew. Cesario's I statements are often antitheses. These include: 'I am not that I play' (1.5.179); and, again to Olivia, 'you are not what you are ... . I am not what I am' (3.1. 137–9). Because antithesis at its best uses the same grammar to articulate opposing ideas, Cesario's more complicated antitheses best capture this rhetorical device. To Olivia, Cesario says 'What I am and what I would are as secret as maidenhead: to your ears, divinity; to any other's, profanation' (1.5.209–11). To Orsino, he confides, 'I am all the daughters of my father's house, / And all the brothers too' (2.4.120–1). Like so much of what Cesario says, these are paradoxes, as we will discuss below. But they are also examples of antithesis.

Apostrophe: The speaker addresses a person who is dead or otherwise not physically present, an imaginary person or a god, an object, place or concept as if the object of address were both physically present and capable of under-standing and responding (Murfin and Ray 210). Examples in *Twelfth Night* include Malvolio's 'Jove, I thank thee' (2.5.172); Olivia's 'Fate, show thy force, ourselves we do not owe / What is decreed must be – and be this so' (1.5.303–4); and Viola/Cesario's 'O time, thou must untangle this, not I. / It is too hard a knot for me t' untie' (2.2.40–41). In this last example, observe how Cesario plays on the homonym knot / not. The 'knot' is both the complications created by trans-vestism, the 'virgin knot', a way of describing the hymen or 'maidenhead', and the fact that Cesario is 'not' a man and does 'not' have that 'little thing' that would make him one. When Cesario imagines what he would do were he to woo Olivia, he concludes that he would 'make the babbling gossip of the air / Cry out "Olivia!"' (1.5.265–6). He thus imagines that he would compel the air itself into apostrophe.

Hyperbole: Exaggeration for emphasis. One sixteenth-century scholar of rhetoric personified hyperbole as the 'over reacher' and the 'loud liar' (Puttenham 319). Sometimes hyperbole is used to express powerful feeling. It was a convention of love poetry. We see it used in this way between Antonio and Sebastian when Antonio says 'If you will not murder me for my love, let me be your servant' and Sebastian replies 'If you will not undo what you have done, that is kill him whom you have recovered, desire it not' (2.1.32–5). But in *Twelfth Night* it is also often used to send up or deflate excessive statements of feeling. Cesario greets Olivia as 'Most radiant, exquisite and unmatchable beauty' (1.5.165) before he knows who she is and before he has seen her face. Feste acknowledges that many of the characters speak a hyperbolic language for feeling when he, disguised as Sir Topas, tries to exorcize the demon afflicting Malvolio as '"Out, hyperbolical fiend"' (4.2.25).

Metaphor: One of the most fundamental of poetic figures. Just as the word 'trope' derives its meaning from the process of turning a word from one meaning or use to another, so the word metaphor refers to transferring or translating meaning, borrowing or substituting terms to convey a resemblance between two things. You may sometimes hear metaphor described in terms of tenor and vehicle: 'The poet, wishing to characterize or elucidate his subject, or *tenor*, chooses a second image as a *vehicle* for doing so' (McDonald 59). While a simile, as we will see, announces its comparison by using the words 'like' or 'as', the metaphor simply states that one thing *is* another. For example, Feste asserts that Orsino's changeable mind is 'a very opal' (2.4.75), meaning that, just as that stone seems to change color from one moment to the next, from one angle to the next, so Orsino's mood and thoughts shift constantly. Maria calls Malvolio 'the trout that must be caught with tickling' (2.5.19–20).

Sir Andrew draws our attention to what a metaphor is and how it works when Maria's joke confuses him. She grabs his hand and places it on her breast, saying 'bring your hand to th'buttery-bar, and let it drink', and referring to her breast as a kind of dairy bar or tap. He asks in response, 'What's your metaphor?' (1.3.68–70). When she explains that her metaphor is 'dry', she means both that her wit is dry or ironic and that her breast is dry, at least as far as he is concerned. He misses her meaning on both counts, suggesting that she refers to his hand as dry, and revealing that, while he can ask what her metaphor is, he doesn't really grasp how metaphor works.

In another scene in *Twelfth Night*, Olivia uses metaphors to describe the difference between small concerns and big ones: 'O, you are sick of self-love, Malvolio, and taste with a distempered appetite. To be generous, guiltless, and of free disposition is to take those things for bird-bolts that you deem cannon bullets' (1.5. 86–9). Olivia does not mean to suggest that Malvolio is actually dealing with bird-balls (small shot) or cannon balls. Instead, she describes how he 'takes' things, mistaking bird shot for cannon balls, little nuisances for deadly force and so blowing things out of proportion. She also describes his character in terms of a 'distempered appetite' that leads him to taste experience, and not just food, but to find it off where others would not. Diagnosing a kind of sickness in him, she also counsels its antidote or cure: a 'generous, guiltless, and free disposition'.

Metonymy: One thing is represented by another that is commonly and often physically associated with it. An often repeated example of metonymy is referring to a monarch as 'the crown' or the monarchy as a 'throne'. Metonymy also substitutes qualities or causes of things for the things themselves. We looked at 'sound' in Orsino's opening speech and the fact that some editors want to change it to 'south'. One critic, however, argues that there is no need to alter the Folio text: '*sound* is a simple metonomy, substituting effect (sound of a breeze) for cause (breeze)' (Booth 130). Sir Andrew expresses his longing for Feste's talents through metonymy, saying 'I had rather than forty shillings I had such a leg, and so sweet a breath to sing, as the fool has' (2.3.19–20), by which he means not that he wants Feste's leg or breath but that he wants the dancing and singing abilities he associates with those body parts. Through metonymy, 'hand' can stand for the hand's effect or product – 'handwriting' – and therefore for the author's responsibility for his or her text or for the pledge of the whole person secured through a handshake in a betrothal or contract. The word 'hand' appears 27 times in *Twelfth Night*, according to the online concordance. In some instances, the 'hand' stands for handwriting, central to the Malvolio plot and the 'martial hand' Sir Toby advises Andrew he needs to write the challenge to Cesario. It also means the pledge that constitutes betrothal: Olivia's 'Give me your hand, sir' to Cesario (3.1.92) and Orsino's request to Cesario 'Give me thy hand' (5.1.268) as well as his offer 'Here is my hand' (5.1.319). When the Priest enters in the final scene to confirm that Olivia and Sebastian are married, he testifies that they confirmed their 'contract of eternal bond of love' by means of 'mutual joinder of your hands' and by 'the holy close of lips' (5.1.152–4). Here the hands and lips stand for the actions and intentions with which they are associated (clasping and kissing), and for the person as a whole who thereby binds him or herself in marriage.

As the hand stands for the whole person it slides from metonymy to its related figure, synecdoche, discussed below. A common example of synecdoche is the phrase 'all hands on deck', meaning all sailors. The difference between metonymic and synecdochic uses of 'hand' is that in the instances of metonymy in *Twelfth Night*, the hand (or leg or breath) does not stand for the whole person as much as it does for the actions associated with that body part or their outcomes (handwriting, handshaking). But there is certainly overlap between the two figures. When Cesario says of Olivia 'methought her eyes had lost her tongue' (2.2.20), he both reduces Olivia to sense organs – suggesting that those body parts can stand for Olivia as a whole person – and describes those organs as at war. The sight of Cesario rendered Olivia speechless. Cesario uses the body parts to refer to the senses with which they are associated (sight and speech) which is more metonymy than synecdoche. While the overlap between metonymy and synecdoche can be confusing, even annoying, it leads you to reflect on relationships between parts and whole, causes and effects.

You could argue that the use of props and furniture on Shakespeare's stage depends on synecdoche. A bed stands for a private chamber even if nothing else is brought on stage; a table brings us to an alehouse or a banquet; a throne creates a palace; a box-tree evokes a garden. Finally, one could argue that Cesario's suit and Viola's maiden's weeds are metonyms – they are associated with each character and come to stand for the two different identities. We will return to this issue – that is, the connection between imagery and plot – in the next chapter.

Oxymoron: Two opposite or apparently contradictory words together. The oxymoron was a favourite trope in Petrarchan love poetry, which sought to articulate the extremes of emotion a lover experienced, the pain of loving and the pleasure of that pain. It is not surprising, then, that oxymorons appear in the play to describe Orsino's love for Olivia. First, Cesario describes Orsino's love to Olivia as 'a deadly life' (1.5.257). Later, Orsino presents his oxymoronic love as a model for Cesario:

> If ever thou shalt love,
> In the sweet pangs of it remember me;
> For such as I am all true lovers are,
> Unstaid and skittish in all motions else,
> Save in the constant image of the creature
> That is beloved. (2.4.15–20)

Not only is 'sweet pangs' an oxymoron, but the rest of Orsino's description of being inconstant about everything but the constant image of his beloved also depends on bringing opposites together, even if in a less direct and concise way.

Paradox: An apparently contradictory or even illogical statement that turns out to be true. Cesario is, in many ways, a walking paradox. He tries to be honest about this, advising Olivia, for instance, that 'I am not that I play' (1.5.179) and 'I am not what I am' (3.1.139).

Parison: Phrases or clauses of equal structure, balanced against one another so that we notice noun corresponding to noun, verb to verb (Keller 275). An example in *Twelfth Night* is the line-up of verbs at the start of each line of this famous passage:

> *Make* me a willow cabin at your gate
> And *call* upon my soul within the house;
> *Write* loyal cantons of contemned love
> And *sing* them loud even in the dead of night;
> *Hallow* your name to the reverberate hills

And *make* the babbling gossip of the air
Cry out 'Olivia!' (1.5.260–6)

Placing a verb near the start of each line, Cesario emphasizes how active his courtship would be – far more active
than that in which Orsino is engaged. In doing so, he goes
far beyond the part he has memorized and exposes Orsino's
own inactivity and detachment (Traub, *Desire and Anxiety*
130). He also defines love as something one does as much as
or more than something one feels. But the action of loving
is, in this speech, largely verbal (calling, writing, singing
hallowing). What's more, Cesario downplays the subject of
these verbs, the 'I' who would do all this for love, in order to
position himself as the object of Olivia's affection, building to
the claim that 'you should not rest … / But you should pity
me' (1.5.266–8). Through the manipulation of grammar here,
Cesario 'is improbably both taking control and disappearing'
(Mallin 205).

Simile: Compares two things, signalling the comparison
with the words 'like' or 'as'. In passages we have discussed
at length, Orsino's desires pursue him 'like fell and cruel
hounds' and Olivia vows to withdraw from the world 'like
a cloistress'. Because the simile reminds us it is making a
comparison, it also alerts us that the two things, while similar,
are not exactly the same. It also reminds us of the writer's or
speaker's role in crafting the comparison.

Synecdoche: Infers qualities of the whole from those of
a part or allows parts to represent wholes. We touched on
the relationship between metonymy and synecdoche above.
Synecdoche is a subset of metonymy. When Cesario says of
Feste that the clown must 'like the haggard, check at every
feather / That comes before his eye' (3.1.62–3), he uses
'feather' to refer to bird. The man wise enough to play the
fool must react to everything he sees, so he is like a haggard
or wild hawk, who starts at any potential prey it comes across.
Note that this instance of synecdoche is also a simile, that is, a
comparison signalled by 'like' or 'as'. A fool is like a haggard.

Shakespeare uses other rhetorical figures, of course, many more. The ones I've listed here are all good ones to get under your belt, as well as figures that Shakespeare relies upon in *Twelfth Night*. The goal here is to develop a vocabulary for discussing Shakespeare's language and the bravery to wade into its multiple meanings. A treasure hunt for images will not get you far. For example, if you do an internet search for particular figures in Shakespeare, you will often come up with poorly chosen examples and misleading definitions. Even scholars can disagree about which names to use for the different tropes and about how to categorize particular instances of wordplay. I am not offering you certainty here, then, but rather encouraging you to embrace an informed uncertainty. As one critic puts it, attending to wordplay can seem like 'an unsettling kind of game' because it undermines our attempts to fix a clear and certain meaning (Ferguson 78). That's precisely what makes it a game. Like Shakespeare and his characters, we are playing with words. Looking more closely at a trope is like pushing on a button: it opens out rather than shutting down or closing off meaning. That's the point and the pleasure. Pay attention to the figures that catch your eye and ear and then follow them as they lead you more deeply into the play's meanings and the words' playfulness.

If you want to write a paper on tropes, 1.5 might make a good focus because it includes so many. Why might that be? What about the characters and their business generates figuration? Your goal is not just to notice, list and name figures but to think about the effects produced by means of these figures.

CHAPTER TWO

Language, character and plot

Shakespeare's characters often speak with distinctive voices, so that we can tell Malvolio from Sir Toby, Olivia from Feste. At one level, the familiar testing practise of asking students to identify the speaker of a given speech should come easily. If we know the play well, we should be able to tell who is speaking and when in the play. Certainly, when we look in depth at a speech we should begin with the questions of who the speaker is and to whom he or she is speaking.

After our discussion at the start of the last chapter, for example, you should be able to identify Orsino's speech as the first in the play and Orsino as the speaker. The speech sets the tone of the play and helps to capture who Orsino is and what we can expect of him in the play – even more than visual cues on stage, such as what he wears, how he looks and moves, will do. But despite all this, there are several important passages in *Twelfth Night* that many students struggle to pin to the correct speakers. This is, in part, because the speeches either express a surprising change in a speaker's attitude or reveal something new about him or her or because the use of pronouns is confusing. As we have already seen, using pronouns in your own writing about this play requires some thought. Is it Viola/she or Cesario/he or Cesario s/he? One of the basic concerns of style is aligning nouns and their pronouns correctly, so that a singular noun takes a singular pronoun (the student … he; the students … they). Trying to avoid gendering pronouns sometimes leads writers to mismatch a singular noun with a plural pronoun, reaching for 'they' because it is ungendered. While common, this is not correct. It is also important that the antecedent of a pronoun is clear. What do you mean by it? Whom do you mean by they? Attending to pronouns with vague antecedents can often help you sharpen your thinking. What precisely do you mean? This is where a basic reading skill and a basic writing skill can reinforce one another. Pay attention to pronouns and antecedents in your writing and in Shakespeare's.

Speakers and their speeches: Pronouns and conditionals in 2.4 and 5.1

Pronouns are one way into the two tricky passages in the play we'll now discuss. In preparation for examining the first (2.4), it is useful to review those moments in the play when we think that Viola speaks as Viola rather than as Cesario. What clues make us think that we are hearing Viola speak from the heart? Need we assume that Viola is the core or authentic self and Cesario just a role she plays? One clue to speech presented to us as reliable self-expression is the first person pronoun. When Cesario speaks as 'I' many are inclined to believe that he is speaking the truth of his/her experience. In exchanges with Olivia, for instance, Cesario asserts that 'I am not what I am' (3.1.139) (note that he says 'am' rather than 'seem' here [Belsey, 'Disrupting' 185]). He also says 'I have one heart, one bosom, and one truth, / And that no woman has, nor never none / Shall mistress be of it, save I alone' (3.1.156–8). In these paradoxical 'I' statements, Cesario asserts a unified self – one heart, one bosom and one truth – but also hints at the division between the self who is speaking (I) and the self described (a woman, a mistress). S/he also utters statements that separate his situation 'As I am a man' from her situation 'As I am a woman' (2.2.36–8). Cesario tells Olivia and the audience that he is speaking in the first person and asserting the truth. But he also frankly asserts that his 'I' is deceptive, inaccessible, mysterious.

Conventionally, dramatic characters advise us that they are speaking the truth when they speak in asides or in soliloquies. Both are forms of direct address to the audience. In the aside, a character turns from the other characters on the stage to make a remark to the audience. This is like speaking directly to the camera. Modern editions sometimes indicate asides with a stage direction *(aside)*. The First Folio did not. So actors can choose whether to act as if an utterance is audible to other characters on stage or not. In a soliloquy, a character is alone and speaks directly to the audience, as if talking to herself or himself out loud. Exits, rather than stage directions, mark a given speech as a soliloquy so one has to pay close attention. It is easy to miss this when reading, but recognizing that a character is alone on stage can influence our interpretation of what he or she has to say. At the end of 1.4, Cesario laments, 'Whoe'er I woo, myself would be his wife' (1.4.42). In this statement, he advises us that he loves Orsino and would like to marry him, rather than wooing Olivia for him. This is information that we would not otherwise know.

It is a theatrical convention to believe information offered to us in this direct way. Cesario says of Feste: 'This fellow is wise enough to play the fool / And to do that well craves a kind of wit' (3.1.58–9) and then proceeds to use the simile comparing the fool to the haggard, which we discussed under synecdoche at the end of the last chapter. Cesario delivers this speech after Feste exits and while he is alone on stage. For many readers and viewers, Cesario's appreciation for Feste, especially since it is not articulated for Feste's benefit, suggests a link of sympathy and function between the two characters. (The Clown or Feste also resembles Viola in that his name is largely withheld from us. The Folio identifies him in speech prefixes as Clo. or Clown. He is named only once in the play, when Curio describes him to Orsino as 'Feste the jester, my lord, a fool that the Lady Olivia's father took much delight in' but who is not quite Olivia's. He is the singer who sang to Orsino 'last night' and who is the next day 'about' Orsino's house and again available to sing for him [2.4.11–13].)

While we are talking about pronouns, it might be useful to consider second person pronouns, that is, those pronouns through which we directly address others. In the early modern period, there were still two forms of second person address. 'Thou' was more familiar than 'you'. It might indicate intimacy or condescension or both. That is, one used it for lovers and family members, but also children, servants and social inferiors. Many critics have pointed out that Olivia addresses Cesario as 'you' when they first meet in 1.5, but that after Cesario leaves, Olivia, alone, discusses him as 'thou': 'I'll be sworn thou art ... give thee fivefold blazon' (1.5.283–5). By 3.1, Olivia is comfortably calling Cesario 'thou'. Sir Toby draws attention to the use of 'thou' when he advises Sir Andrew to refer to Cesario as 'thou' in his challenge to him: 'If thou thou'st him some thrice, it shall not be amiss' (3.2.42–3). By himself referring to Sir Andrew as 'thou', Sir Toby both performs an intimacy with him and asserts his own superiority. Sir Andrew, 'evidently somewhat in awe of Sir Toby, never ventures to return his intimate *thou*' (Adamson 229). It's worth searching pronouns using a searchable text or concordance in order to see who addresses whom as 'thou' in the play and to reflect on what that seems to mean.

Act 2, scene 4

Now let's turn to an exchange between Orsino and Cesario in which Cesario does and does not express his feelings and Viola's. In 2.4, Orsino urges Cesario to return to the project of wooing Olivia. Cesario wonders what will happen if Olivia simply cannot be wooed. (Note that Orsino proposes something like a disregard for her consent when he urges Cesario 'to leap all civil bounds' in pressing his suit to Olivia [1.4.21]. Could this be linked to the Lucrece references, by which Maria and Malvolio associate Olivia with a rape victim?). Mustn't Orsino take no for an answer? Cesario dares to challenge Orsino here, questioning his generalizations and his course of action in demanding a response from Olivia that she cannot and will not give. Cesario raises the example of 'some lady' who might love Orsino as much as he loves Olivia. Wouldn't she have to take no for an answer? Already, Cesario is both discussing a hypothetical lady in love with Orsino and him/herself. Orsino responds by claiming that a woman could not love as much as he does; there is no parallel between his love and the love that women can experience. This bold assertion tempts Cesario to counter Orsino's presumption to speak for all women and to articulate knowledge based on experience: 'Ay, but I know—' Cesario ventures. 'What dost thou know?' Orsino prompts.

Cesario must then defend women's capacity to love based on his experience while also explaining how he can have access to this experience. He claims to know

> Too well what love women to men may owe.
> In faith, they are as true of heart as we.
> My father had a daughter loved a man,
> As it might be, perhaps, were I a woman,
> I should your lordship.
> DUKE ORSINO: And what's her history?
> VIOLA: A blank, my lord. She never told her love,
> But let concealment, like a worm i' th' bud
> Feed on her damask cheek. She pined in thought,
> And with a green and yellow melancholy
> She sat like Patience on a monument,
> Smiling at grief. Was not this love indeed?
> We men may say more, swear more, but indeed
> Our shows are more than will, for still we prove
> Much in our vows, but little in our love.

DUKE ORSINO: But died thy sister of her love, my boy?
VIOLA: I am all the daughters of my father's house,
And all the brothers too; and yet I know not.
Sir, shall I to this lady? (105–22)

This is a complicated exchange and one much discussed by
critics. There are a number of ways of getting a handle on this
speech – and to get a handle simply means identifying where
the action is rather than resolving the ambiguities that animate
the exchange. First, we've talked about how scenes are named.
This one is often called the 'Patience on a monument' scene
after the simile Cesario uses. His sister sat 'like Patience on
a monument'. This is sometimes described as an instance
of personification, the figure by which an abstraction is
described as a person. But that is not quite what is happening
here. Cesario describes his sister as *like* the *statue* on a tomb
representing patience, 'smiling at grief', or enduring it. So he
describes his sister, who is also himself, as turned to stone,
inanimate, in a cemetery. It's a vivid image of an unspoken,
unfulfilled love leading to death or as itself a kind of death.
How else might you identify the scene? Note, too, that while
Cesario speaks most of the lines here, this is a conversation
more than a speech. Orsino asks two questions prompting
Cesario's response. The first one is an example of how two
characters work together to form one line of verse. Orsino's
'And what's her history?' completes the line Cesario begins.
The speech then ends with Cesario's question, a version of
'what now?' In between, questions move the exchange along.
'What dost thou know?' 'And what's her history?' 'Was not
this love indeed?' 'But died thy sister of her love, my boy?'
'Sir, shall I to this lady?' We can read this exchange as tracing
an arc from asserting knowledge to becoming doubtful of
that knowledge: moving from Cesario's 'I know' to Orsino's
question 'what do you know?' to Cesario's concluding 'I know
not'.

Just as isolating the questions or the repetition of the word
'know' helps us understand the exchange more deeply, so

highlighting the **pronouns** helps us grasp the complexity of Cesario's position and of the intelligence he confides. Cesario presents his sister as a third person whose story he can tell (my father's man-loving daughter/ she/ her). He also identifies with the men Orsino has generalized about (We men/ our vows/ our love) as opposed to the women he undertakes to defend ('they are as true of heart as we'). If Cesario is consistent in playing out his role as male confidante, identifying with other men as 'we' while defending women's capacity for love ('they'), his articulation of a first person towards the end of the exchange – 'I am all the daughters of my father's house, / And all the brothers too' – unsettles that opposition. Cesario is the 'we' and the 'they', the 'I' and the 'she'. He tells his sister's story and his own. As one critic puts it,

> Viola's history is the play we are watching, which is certainly not a blank but packed with events. Nor is it true that she never told her love. She has already told it once in this scene [2.4.107–9, lines 3–5 in the passage as quoted above], and she is here telling it again in hints so broad that even Orsino is able to pick them up once he has one more clue,

which he gets in the final scene when he learns that Cesario is Viola (Belsey, 'Disrupting' 187). The speech only makes sense if we grasp that 'the Viola who speaks is not identical to the Viola she speaks of' (187); in addition, as I would put it, Cesario is not the same as Viola, and the Viola described is not exactly the Viola who plays the part of Cesario. The history he recounts is one possible story for Viola – not what has happened or what will but what could, if Viola's love remains unspoken and unreciprocated.

Like pronouns, **tense** is a basic yet crucial consideration in both critical reading and effective writing. Teachers will often advise you to 'use tenses consistently'. The tense of a verb alerts the reader to whether an action has happened in the past, is happening in the present or will happen in the future.

But Cesario moves around in time in a fascinating way in this exchange. We move from the present tense description of how women are – always and everywhere – to the past tense – my father had a daughter who loved a man – to a prediction of what could happen. As one critic puts it,

> Viola's parable of her imaginary sister who 'never told her love' creates a temporary suspension of the flow of time in the play as she looks backward to an imagined past which is at the same time an image of the future that she fears for herself, for she cannot tell whether her imaginary sister died of her grief; but she jolts herself out of her reverie

by committing herself to action in the present (Wells 182). Even the key line that gives this scene its name combines simple past tense with a continuous present tense in the participle smiling: 'She *sat* like Patience on a monument, / *Smiling* at grief' (2.4.114–15).

The **mood** of the verbs is as interesting as their shifting tenses. If tense addresses the *when* of a verb's action, mood conveys the *how*. Verb moods include indicative, imperative, infinitive and subjunctive. In this scene, I want to draw attention to the subjunctive mood, in part because it is a key mood in this play. The subjunctive mood expresses conditionals or possibilities, that is, 'ifs'. As Cesario puts it: 'As it *might be*, perhaps, *were* I a woman, / I *should* your lordship'. Describing how it might be, Cesario also describes how it is (she is a woman and does love Orsino) and how she wishes it could be (if she could reveal herself to be a woman, express that love and have it reciprocated). Conditionals are often important in *Twelfth Night*. Cesario often depicts himself as inhabiting someone else's subject position. After Orsino advises him not to take no for an answer from Olivia, Cesario takes the advice one step further imagining how it would feel to be Orsino and how he would act. Inhabiting the possibility of loving Olivia passionately, he tells her: 'If I did love you in my master's flame, / such a suffering, such a deadly life, / In your denial I would find no sense; / I would not understand it' (1.5.256–9). Whereas Olivia ignores Orsino's refusal to take no for an answer, she is captivated by Cesario's insistence that *if he* loved her, he *could* not do so; he *would* have no choice. Cesario's conditional strikes her as a declaration of love; he seduces her into imagining him as a lover. Cesario's use of the conditional here should not be taken as any less authentic, any more a performance, than the claim we've just considered that *if* Cesario *were* a woman he *would* love Orsino as much as his sister loved a man (Traub, *Desire and Anxiety* 131–2).

When evaluating any scene or speech, it's useful to contemplate what it accomplishes in the play. That is, what has changed by the end? What have we learned that we didn't know before? In the 'Patience on a monument' scene, what prompts Cesario/Viola to speak? Does s/he get what s/he wants? Is it in his or her best interests? Some take Cesario's last line – 'Sir, shall I to this lady?' as a change of subject. But it's also true that Cesario simply returns to the subject with which the conversation started, Orsino's pursuit of Olivia. Upon hearing Cesario's defence of women's love, Orsino recommits to his wooing of Olivia – 'To her in haste' (2.4.123). Defending women's capacity for love, Cesario has both defended Viola's passion and undermined it by insisting that her rival Olivia is capable of love and thus worth pursuing. At this moment, Cesario has, by telling his sister's/her own story, goaded Orsino on. He must now rouse himself to try again to woo Olivia – and to fend off her advances toward him.

Act 5, scene 1

Let's now turn to a moment much later in the play, in its last scene. This is another speech that, in my experience, students have a hard time identifying correctly. Who says this to whom about whom? Here again, one of the things that makes the speech challenging is also an entry point to its meanings: the pronouns. In the last scene of the play, we see Olivia and

Orsino together for the first time. She rejects him decisively. He expresses his disappointment and rage in this speech:

> Why should I not, had I the heart to do it,
> Like to th'Egyptian thief at point of death,
> Kill what I love – a savage jealousy
> That sometime savours nobly? But hear me this:
> Since you to non-regardance cast my faith,
> And that I partly know the instrument
> That screws me from my true place in your favour,
> Live you the marble-breasted tyrant still.
> But this your minion, whom I know you love,
> And whom, by heaven I swear, I tender dearly,
> Him will I tear out of that cruel eye,
> Where he sits crowned in his master's spite. (5.1.113–24)

Presented out of context, this speech stumps many readers. The opening simile and allusion ('like to th'Egyptian thief') confuses rather than clarifies for most readers. One has to look at the note to understand the allusion to Thyamis, an Egyptian 'king of thieves' who tried to kill his beloved captive when his own life was threatened by a rival band but who failed to do so. The point of the simile – killing what you love – is clear even if one doesn't know the story, but recognizing the allusion alerts the listener or reader that Thyamis did not in fact kill his beloved captive. Furthermore, what do you make of the conditional question 'why should I not, had I the heart to do it'? Is Orsino wishing he had the heart to kill but knowing he doesn't? Is he saying here that he knows he could never do this? Or is he expressing momentary doubt, reflecting on what it would take to carry through, and then moving forward with the plan?

Who is being addressed as the 'marble-breasted tyrant'? Who is 'the instrument' and 'your minion'? On stage, it's clear that Orsino is speaking to Olivia and talking about Cesario, for whom he expresses love and whom he identifies, for the first time, as his rival for Olivia's affections. But on the page, it can be difficult to identify the players, since Orsino refers to himself in the first person – there are many I's in this speech – but also in the third, as 'his master'. Orsino's rage also strikes many readers as a surprise. Is this the languid, lovesick man of the first scene? Many misidentify the speaker as Malvolio, simply because they identify Malvolio with rage and threats of revenge. Orsino's words also echo those of Antonio. Antonio's rage at Cesario in 3.4 anticipates Orsino's rage at Cesario at the end of the play. Just as Orsino responds violently to disappointment in the woman (and perhaps the boy) he has idealized, so Antonio claims that he worshipped Sebastian as an idol or god and so experiences rejection by him as deep disillusionment, spiritual as well as erotic. Antonio explains his devotion to Sebastian with an inversion of usual word order that often bewilders students: 'And to his image, which methought did promise / Most venerable worth, did I devotion' (3.4.359–60). We might reorder this: 'And I did devotion to his image, which I thought promised most venerable worth'. To understand the lines we have to rearrange the words in our heads. Yet Antonio's word order in the play has its own virtues. He leads with Sebastian's image, which he also describes as what drew him, what determined his response and compelled his devotion. And he ends with the word describing his own relation to Sebastian's image, the relationship he laments here.

One of the pleasures of Shakespeare's language is that he alternates lines that seem challenging and old school with ones that sound as if someone might casually toss them off today. This scene (3.4) includes one such. The First Officer who is arresting Antonio interrupts to say: 'What's that to us?' Antonio wants to explain why he is in Illyria and why it is so outrageous to be denied by the man whose life he's saved. To the officers, this is irrelevant. But Antonio goes on to emphasize 'how vile an idol' the man he worshipped as a god has turned out to be. He returns to the issue of appearances. Sebastian has shamed his 'good feature' or physical attractiveness by revealing himself as morally unattractive.

The result is an oxymoron and a paradox: 'beauteous evil'. Unkindness is the true deformity, Antonio concludes. He shouldn't have fallen for a beautiful outside (3.4.356–367). Antonio has mistaken Cesario for Sebastian. But what are we to make of the fact that Cesario/Sebastian is the target of both these attacks?

Let's return to the last scene. This moment is challenging and it goes by quickly. But it is worth lingering over it. Orsino proposes a plan of action to get back at Olivia. The plan is to prevent her from having Cesario, whom Orsino acknowledges, at this moment, that they both love. He then heads offstage with Cesario:

> Come, boy, with me. My thoughts are ripe in mischief.
> I'll sacrifice the lamb that I do love
> To spite a raven's heart within a dove. (124–7)

Again, identifying the players can be tricky – in this case both on stage and on the page. Who is the lamb, who the raven and who the dove? The lamb is Cesario, who is also the boy. Olivia is the dove – but she harbours a raven's heart. The bottom line is that Orsino threatens to kill Cesario and Cesario appears to submit to death at his hand. We are on the brink of tragedy here. What are the effects of bringing us to the edge of this cliff just before resolving (most of) the crises? What clues does the play give us – into Orsino's character, for instance – that help us interpret this moment? Are there any other ways in which the play is brought so close to violence and death?

It isn't only Orsino's 'mischief' and murderous intent that bring this scene to a crisis. Cesario follows Orsino and claims he loves him more than life, more than wife – an assertion to which Olivia, understandably, objects. Olivia then reveals her marriage to Cesario (really Sebastian), prompting more rage from Orsino, who turns on Cesario as a 'dissembling cub', again disparaging a human who disappoints him as an animal, and vowing never to meet Cesario again. Critic Penny Gay points out the functions of rhyme in this climactic scene starting with l.126 'I'll sacrifice the lamb that I do love' ('*Twelfth*' 437). Orsino first admits love for Cesario. In the next 14 lines, notice how two characters sometimes share a line. The sharing works as follows: Olivia and Cesario ('Where goes Cesario? After him I love') and then Olivia and Orsino ('Call forth the holy father. Come, away') followed by Orsino and Olivia ('Husband? Ay, husband') and finally Orsino and Cesario ('Her husband, sirrah? No, my lord, not I'). In this rapid back-and-forth dialogue, we hear mounting tension, the repetition of the word 'love', including five lines ending with 'love' or rhymes on it, and the splitting apart of Olivia and Cesario and Olivia and Orsino in the service of transforming Orsino and Olivia into in-laws and allies and coupling Orsino and Cesario.

Language and plot

The two speeches on which we've focused in this chapter help shape our impressions of the characters of Orsino and Viola/Cesario and enhance our understanding of their relationship, their attitudes toward one another and their love. Although it can be hard to attach these speeches to their speakers, the speeches, in fact, help to create the speakers. In *Twelfth Night*, language isn't only tied to character. It is also interwoven tightly with plot. Some revisions of Shakespeare plays (such as the *Shakespeare Re-told* series or paraphrases) might suggest that the plot is a kind of scaffold or skeleton that is then dressed in the language and can be redressed without fundamental alteration. But in this play, as in many others, events in the play inform the language. Let us trace just two strands of many: the sea and twins. For example, the shipwreck that brings both Viola and Sebastian to Illyria, thus launching the double romance plot at the centre of the play, lingers in images of water and weeping, as when Olivia waters her chamber daily 'with eye-offending brine' so as to cure her memory of her dead brother as one might cure a foodstuff in salt. Sebastian tells Antonio of Viola: 'She is drowned already, sir, with salt water, though I seem to drown her remembrance again with more' (2.1.28–9). But if Sebastian thinks the sea has taken his twin, he also cast himself afloat on it, binding himself to a mast so that he could 'hold acquaintance with the waves' (1.2.15). This ability to float, and to make friends with an element rather than oppose what Hamlet calls 'a sea of troubles', will then prove characteristic of Sebastian in his relation to Illyria and to Olivia. Sebastian may wonder 'how runs the stream?' in this mad world in which Olivia acts as if she knows and loves him, but he goes with the flow.

The play begins with Orsino's discussion of how the spirit of love 'receiveth as the sea' by which he seems to mean that it is endlessly capacious but also overwhelming – whatever it receives soon 'falls into abatement and low price' (1.1.11–13). The sea is a confusing metaphor in this speech, functioning 'both as a massive reservoir of emotional intensity, which the storm recapitulates in the next scene, and also as a fundamentally imperturbable thing, unchanged by additions or abatements' (Mentz 58). Feste tells Orsino his mind is an opal and that he would have men of 'such constancy put to sea, that their business might be everything and their intent everywhere' – that is, they would be upon the element as changeable as they are (2.4.75–7). Orsino insists his love, compared to women's 'is all as hungry as the sea, / And can digest as much' (2.4.100–1). Viola describes Olivia as 'the list of my voyage' (3.1.74–5). Fabian warns Sir Andrew 'you are now sailed into the north of my lady's opinion' because of Cesario (3.2.24–5). Finally, Orsino says 'I shall have share in this most happy wreck' in 5.1. Thus, the sea is both a setting, since Illyria is on the coast, an event (the storm and wreck that bring the twins to Illyria), and a pervasive pattern of imagery. It also connects to references to piracy in the play. These extend beyond the accusation that Antonio is a pirate, which he refutes, to include Sir Toby's definition of the word 'accost' – the basic meaning of which is address or approach in order to speak to – as 'front her, board her, woo her, assail her' (1.3.54–5). Sir Toby thus links women and ships, courtship and piracy, desire and theft.

The play's main plot revolves around twins and the mistaken identities they generate. But other doublings proliferate around the twins. Doublings in the play include two clowns (Feste and Malvolio); two romantic/ Petrarchan lovers (Orsino and Sir Andrew); two boys (Cesario and Sebastian); two sea captains (or is it one captain and a pirate?); two ladies of the house (Olivia and her agent, Maria, whose handwriting can easily be mistaken for hers); and two priests (the real one and Sir Topas) (Gay, '*Twelfth*' 439). Cesario and Sebastian are both forced into duelling with Sir Andrew and both give money to Feste (Lewalski 174). We also have, by the end, other multiples: three couples and three jilted lovers (Malvolio, Antonio, Andrew). As we have seen in the list of rhetorical figures at the end of the last chapter, the confusion the twins cause is figured rhetorically in a range of tropes that depend on repetition, doubling, and mirroring. Let me here add three more such figures. One is **hysteron proteron**, by which the last comes first. An example of this is when the Captain tells Viola he knows Illyria because he was 'bred and born / Not three hours' travel from this very place' (1.2.20–1). We would expect him to say born and bred because that is the sequence in which the events occurred. **Hendiadys** creates another kind of rhetorical twinning. Hendiadys uses two nouns connected by 'and' rather than combining an adjective and noun, as would be more common. The rhetorician George Puttenham calls hendiadys 'the figure of twins' because through it 'you will seem to make two of one' (Puttenham 188). An example in the play is Sebastian's reference to 'this accident and flood of fortune' (4.3.11) rather than 'this accidental flood of fortune'. The play's final scene can be read as a kind of visualization or embodiment of hendiadys: 'the final scene presents the two possibilities of a doubled image (a kind of visual hendiadys) or of two separate images contracted into one (hendiadys in reverse)' (Elam 85). The final scene can also be read as a form

of '**geminatio**', the repetition of the same word with no inter-
vening space. The term comes from the Latin noun for twin
and the verb meaning 'to double'. This figure, too, suggests
how plot and figuration intertwine in *Twelfth Night*.

Writing matters

Pairing texts

One trigger for your own writing might be to pursue the
approach we've just been taking, linking image clusters and
rhetorical figures to the plot. Can you find other ways in
which the sea or twinning and doubling shape both language
and action? How about other connections between events
and imagery? Love and death are other possibilities. In the
first chapter, we compared passages in Shakespeare's play to
several other popular genres from the period, including the
carpe diem poem and the blazon. We've also discussed the
fact that this is a play founded on death (Viola's father and
Olivia's father and brother) and the presumption of death
(Viola and Sebastian each thinks the other is dead). Death
forms the play's backstory – freeing the young people to make
their own matches, taking Olivia's brother and miring her in
mourning, and claiming Viola's brother too, at least as she
thinks.

In order to think more deeply about death as event and
backstory but also as theme and image, you might try pairing
part of *Twelfth Night* with part of a script that is arguably one
of the most familiar and widely performed in the period, the
Elizabethan Book of Common Prayer. This volume recommended scriptural readings and established the scripts for
worship services and for common rituals such as marriage,
baptism and burial in the Church of England. In the 1559
version of the Book of Common Prayer, 'The Order for the
Burial of the Dead' explains that when the mourners arrive at

the graveside, and while the 'corpse is made ready to be laid into the earth', the priest should say or sing this passage, the first lines of which come from the Book of Job 14:

> MAN that is born of a woman hath but a short time to live, and is full of misery. He cometh up and is cut down like a flower; he flieth as it were a shadow, and never continueth in one stay. In the midst of life we be in death: of whom may we seek for succour but of thee, O Lord, which for our sins justly art displeased. Yet, O Lord God most holy, O Lord most mighty, O holy and most merciful savior, deliver us not into the bitter pains of eternal death. Thou knowest, Lord, the secrets of our hearts, shut not up thy merciful eyes to our prayers: but spare us Lord most holy, O God most mighty, O holy and merciful savior, thou most worthy judge eternal, suffer us not at our last hour for any pains of death to fall from thee.

Then while bystanders throw dirt upon the corpse, the priest is directed to say:

> FORASMUCH as it hath pleased Almighty God of his great mercy to take unto himself the soul of our dear brother here departed: we therefore commit his body to the ground, earth to earth, ashes to ashes, dust to dust, in sure and certain hope of resurrection to eternal life, through our Lord Jesus Christ, who shall change our vile body that it may be like to his glorious body, according to the mighty working, whereby he is able to subdue all things to himself.
> (*Book of Common Prayer* 310)

Compare this crucial moment of the funeral service with moments when Olivia and Viola discuss their grief for their dead brothers, particularly the exchange between Feste and Olivia in 1.5. First, what are the implications of viewing both of these texts as scripts for performance? How is this different, for example, from viewing one, the funeral service from *The*

Book of Common Prayer, as an historical document and the other, the scene from *Twelfth Night*, as a literary text? Second, how are the two similar in their depiction of grief and the appropriate response to it? How do they differ? Identify at least one example of figurative language from each text. How and with what effect does each text use figurative language to capture both the inevitability of mortality and religious faith in resurrection? Do not conclude your comparison without reflecting on how would you name the relationship between your two texts. On the one hand, this is a simple choice of verb. Perhaps you think that the funeral service parallels, resembles, shapes or influences the play, or that the play reflects, quotes or comments on the funeral service, or that the two texts participate in the culture's exploration of Christian grief. There are many possibilities and there is not a right or wrong choice here. But when you choose the verb you want to use you are making a choice about your method and about the relationships you want to suggest between literature and history, representation and performance. In your analysis, the verb you use does a lot of the work of comparing the two texts and explaining why that comparison matters and what kinds of insight it yields.

Playing parts

We began this chapter with a discussion of speeches that many students have a hard time tying to the correct speaker. Another illuminating writing exercise involves breaking the play – or at least part of it – into roles so that you can isolate everything that a particular character says and see what that will teach you about the character and the play. At the very least, it will, like reading scenes aloud, help you pay closer attention to speech prefixes (that is, who is saying what to whom) and to how characters are tied to and created through their words.

This exercise builds on the research of Simon Palfrey and Tiffany Stern. Palfrey and Stern argue that, in Shakespeare's theatre, actors did not receive copies of the whole play in which they'd appear, but rather handwritten scrolls containing just their own part and their cues, that is, the preceding word or two before they were to speak. This scroll did not include what would be said to your character if it wasn't a cue or what was said about you elsewhere in the play. It also did not indicate which character would speak the cues. The part could be fastened to a wooden stick and then rolled around it, which seems to be the source of the word 'role'. The scrolls were easily carried and enabled the actors to focus on their own roles.

Why did this become the standard practise? It helped to protect the theatre company's control over their property: 'the more copies of a play, the more likely it was that one would fall into the hands of either a rival company or a printer' (Palfrey and Stern 1). Paper was also expensive. But above all, this was just the custom, one that lasted for centuries. One of its consequences is that sixteenth- and early seventeenth-century plays do not survive in manuscript. This is not a result of some conspiracy to disguise authorship, as some attempts to claim that someone else wrote Shakespeare's plays suggest. It's a consequence of the fact that plays may never have existed as complete texts. Just as each character's part existed separately, so other parts of plays, including the letters and songs that figure so importantly in a play like *Twelfth Night*, may have circulated separately. The actor playing Malvolio may not have memorized the forged letter as part of his part but rather depended upon reading that letter on stage – although he would have to memorize his many interruptions of and comments on his own reading! Feste's final song in *Twelfth Night* turns up in *King Lear*, sung by a Fool who may first have been played by the same actor who played Feste. Some of the other songs in the play seem to have been borrowed rather than newly composed for the play. Just as the rearrangement of key scenes of the play in production suggests that the play has a modular structure, so the recycling of Feste's song (and perhaps of others) suggests the ways that plays were mobile assemblages of independent, freely circulating pieces.

Dividing and distributing plays as separate parts promoted a theatrical culture in which an actor owned and was identified with his part. He might pass his scroll – and annotations about movements and line delivery – to the next actor to play it. Actors memorized parts on their own rather than through interaction with other players. They probably had only one group rehearsal for a given play and each actor would be preparing for many other plays as well. 'Actors were expected to have upwards of forty roles in their heads or to hand, and might regularly be asked to learn new plays while performing an endless series of old ones' (Palfrey and Stern 76). Hirelings who played minor parts might never have heard the whole play in which they appeared.

How would everyone keep track? There was no director. Instead, a prompter wrote the 'plot' and 'ran' a performance. 'Plots' hung on the wall of the 'tyring house' (the offstage dressing or at-tiring area).

> Divided into two columns, each of which is subdivided into scenes, the plot provides not the story of the play, but the sequence of dramatic events in the play. Specifically, it contains actors' entrances – and some additional details about properties and who else would be on-stage. (Palfrey and Stern 72)

The 'plot' does not necessarily note exits. The posted 'plot' served to help the player, who had rehearsed on his own, to keep track of what was happening in a scene and to map 'his progress through the play in a series of entrances and properties'. Whereas a director now tends to have a 'vision' of the play that guides everything in a production, from design to line readings, the prompter – with the help of his 'plot' – acted more as a stage manager, making sure that the needed actors and props appeared on stage as required. The posted plot made it possible for actors who rehearsed independently to perform collaboratively.

All of this may be historically interesting, but what's it to you? I'm suggesting that you experiment with creating a scroll. Palfrey and Stern have manufactured new evidence from much-studied Shakespeare plays by dividing them into actors' parts, which they call 'imaginatively reconstructed part-scripts'. You can do this too. It might be overwhelming to do this for the whole play. But you can create a part-script for a minor character (such as the Captain) covering the whole play. You can also create a part-script for a major character for just one scene or act. What do you see about the character and his or her words when you isolate them in this way? What do you think you miss? When does the task become difficult (such as when a character is engaging in rapid-fire exchange with another character)?

Creating part scrolls can alert you to a currency actors know well – who gets the most lines? It can be an eye opener. In one famous example, Katharina in *The Taming of the Shrew* gets the longest speech in the play – after she has been tamed. This suggests that one of the things she gains in the taming process is the licence to perform her virtue for others, to stand in the limelight. In *Twelfth Night*, it might surprise you to learn that Sir Toby has more lines than anyone else. 'Toby has 364 lines (16.5 percent of the play) to 339 (13 percent) for Viola, 318 (12 percent) for Feste, 313 (12 percent) for Olivia, and 286 (11 percent) for Malvolio' (Booth 161). You might either defend Toby's monopoly on lines or make an argument for why his part should be cut for performance. You can find information on how many lines a character has at the website https://sites.google.com/a/shakespearelinecount.com/www/shakespeare-characters-line-count. Counts will vary depending on the edition used. Indeed, you will find totals on this site slightly different from those I've just listed.

In those Shakespeare plays that include a fool or clown, that character is often a useful one on which to focus. Like Cesario, Feste is mobile, moving between Olivia's and Orsino's households and equally at home in each. He connects with most of the characters. For example, note how many characters tip him (Cesario, Sebastian, Toby, Sir Andrew and Orsino, but not his mistress, Olivia). He stands outside the conclusion to comment on it and he was portable enough that a character very like him, singing his concluding song, could be moved to another play, *King Lear*. What would be missing if you took Feste out? Why end the play with Feste's song? What is the effect of that? Alternatively, what would be your argument for cutting Feste out of the play?

CHAPTER THREE

Language through time

This chapter focuses on how language changes over time as well as how language enables us to make connections across time – to time travel as it were. We have already discussed how to use the *Oxford English Dictionary*, a Shakespeare Concordance and the *Shakespeare's Words* website in order 1) to examine a word's range of meaning and changes in meaning over time and then 2) use that word or phrase as a portal into the play's larger concerns. We will build on that proceeding here. We will look at a number of words and images in the play whose meanings have been lost or grown dim because of change over time. We cannot always grasp an allusion to a practise that is no longer familiar, or slang that has been outgrown.

Even the smallest words can have meanings that have changed over time. Let's take 'and' as a case in point since it is the kind of 'filler' word we often ignore, assuming that its meaning is self-evident and unchanging. Shakespeare uses 'and' not just as a conjunction but also as an adverb. In the first line of Feste's song at the end of the play, 'When that I was *and* a little tiny boy' (5.1.382), the 'and' adds emphasis as an adverb would and has the sense of 'only'. At the start of sentences, it can mean 'indeed', again adding emphasis. Finally, as a subordinating conjunction it means 'if'. Often, when it is used with this meaning, the First Folio spells it as 'An' (Blake, *Shakespeare's Language*, 115). Some editions modernize this to 'and' and some do not. For example, when Sir Andrew says 'An you love me, let's do't' (2.3.59) he uses 'An' with the meaning of 'if'. The two words frequently combine in the conjunction *and if*, which often bears the stronger meaning of 'if only'. We find the phrase with this meaning in Shakespeare's *As You Like It*, when Phebe challenges Silvius's use of the hyperbole of love poetry by saying 'And if mine eyes can wound, now let them kill thee' (3.5.16). Since we assume we know what 'and' means, it is easy to miss subtle changes in its meaning and use over time. More often, unfamiliar words and allusions grab our attention.

Bears, baiting and other animal imagery

For instance, Shakespeare often refers to the practise of bear-baiting in his plays. Bear baiting was a sport available continuously in London from the twelfth century on. Bear-baiting pits and theatres had a similar circular shape; theatres may even have been modeled on bear-baiting arenas. Theatres and bear-baiting arenas coexisted in the same neighbourhood. Some venues were even used for both enter-tainments. For example, the Hope theatre held both kinds of events on alternating days. A bear-baiting arena could accom-modate 1,000 spectators and admission cost only a penny. A bear was chained to a stake and then whipped and set on by dogs. Some bears had been blinded. Some had had pepper blown up their noses to irritate them. 'The idea was to release the dogs to worry at the chained bears who would then lash out, attacking and killing where they could' (Stern, *Making* 19). Bears usually survived the baitings; many dogs did too. Just as there were actors who were well known, there were bears who were stars, known by name and able to pull in big crowds (Hawkes). When plays in the public theatres were suspended, bear-baitings continued until 1656, at which point several instances of bears killing spectators led to the banning of the sport (Ravelhofer 292, but see Semenza 159).

Shakespeare draws on bear-baiting as a powerful image of the suffering of tragic protagonists, who cannot escape or change their circumstances, but can only endure. In *King Lear*, Gloucester announces that 'I am tied to th'stake, and I must stand the course' (3.7.52). Macbeth says: 'They have tied me to a stake. I cannot fly, / But bear-like I must fight the course' (5.7.1–2). In the metaphor of the tragic protagonist as baited bear, Shakespeare's sympathy 'is wholly on the side of the bear, and he accentuates his bravery and the horror of his position' (Spurgeon 110; see also Callaghan, *Who* 159).

How does such an image work in a comedy? In *Twelfth Night*, when Olivia questions Cesario about the ring she sent after him, she asks:

Have you not set mine honor at the stake
And baited it with all th'unmuzzled thoughts
That tyrannous heart can think? (3.1.116–18)

Here Olivia is not at the stake, but her honour is. Cesario has baited it by unleashing Olivia's own 'unmuzzled thoughts', thoughts, that is, that take the place of the dogs, unmuzzled and so able to nip at the immobilized bear (here Olivia's honour). Fabian reports to Sir Toby that Cesario is as afraid of Sir Andrew as he is of him and 'pants and looks pale as if a bear were at his heels' (3.4.287–8). Orsino's name, which means 'the little bear', might link him to this pattern of imagery as well (Malcolmson 48). Do you see any ways in which Orsino is a bear who is tied to the stake or tormented? Or does he seem predatory? Although most readers now will look to the glosses to understand these references to bears, they would have been more familiar to sixteenth- and seventeenth-century audiences.

We tend to think about going to the theatre as an elite entertainment, because it is so expensive now. Many college students have never seen a live theatrical performance. But thinking about bear-baiting as a rival to the theatre reveals the theatre as more rough-and-tumble than we might imagine.

The same people who went to the theatre might also attend a
bear-baiting in the same week; they would pay about the same
amount and spend about the same time being entertained
(about two hours). 'Plays had to offer an entertainment at least
as compelling as the visceral, bloody, brutal sport of killing or
maiming bears, dogs and bulls' (Stern, *Making* 19). In addition
to animal blood sports, the theatre had to compete with public
punishments too. On scaffolds that looked very much like
stages, felons were beheaded (if they were aristocrats), hanged
(if they were not) or, more gruesomely, disembowelled and
dismembered (if they were convicted of treason). On their
way to the theatres, playgoers might even pass traitors' heads
impaled on spikes. Women accused of killing their husbands
might be burned at the stake, as were religious martyrs in the
sixteenth century. Those convicted of lesser offences might be
placed in pillories, subject to the verbal abuse and garbage
hurled at them by the crowds, or publicly whipped. Huge
crowds gathered for these spectacles. As a result, early modern
people knew what blood and death really looked like. 'Just
as at the bear-garden, audiences at the stocks, the pillory, the
scaffold and the whipping post were not discouraged from
active vocal and even physical participation in the spectacular
harassment of a centrally displayed figure' (Hawkes 90).
Audiences were, then, rowdy, responsive, used to violence and
even antagonistic to the bears, felons, and actors who stood
before them. I'm not advising you to throw things at the stage
or bet on who will still be standing at the play's end. But I do
think that a little irreverence, a little licence to push back, can
enhance your enjoyment.

At the same time, it is worth acknowledging the role that
brutality can play in our pleasure, in Shakespeare as well
as in other forms of media, such as video games, in which
we are more aware of that fact. Several critics argue that
in the sport Maria, Sir Toby and others make of Malvolio,
they put him in the bear's place, baiting and mocking him
(Berry 118–19; Callaghan, *Who?* 154–5). In a 1987 Royal
Shakespeare Company production, Malvolio 'was blindfolded

and whipped, chained to a pole, like a bear being baited' (Gay, 'Introduction' 13), making this imagery explicit. At the end of the play, Malvolio articulates his awareness that he has been baited and his contempt for the pack of dogs who have tormented him when he says 'I'll be revenged on the whole *pack* of you' (5.1.371) (emphasis added). One critic goes so far as to conclude 'that the ultimate effect of *Twelfth Night* is to make the audience ashamed of itself' (Berry 119). If we accept the idea that Shakespeare sympathized with bears, then this would be the connection between comedies and tragedies. Do you think that the bear image invites our sympathy for Malvolio? Does Shakespeare criticize aggressive laughter at Malvolio's expense or exploit it? Is it possible to do both? Since plays were performed in the afternoon and used no artificial lighting, the audience was visible to the players and to one another. We have come to think of ourselves as invisible consumers, absorbed in screens that cannot see us. Imagining that performers can see us and our reactions – as they can in a theatre or lecture hall – holds us more accountable for our responses but can also engage us more closely.

The bear is not the only animal to serve a function in *Twelfth Night*. We have seen the confusing references to the lamb and the raven's heart within a dove in Orsino's speech in the last scene. When Malvolio congratulates himself on winning Olivia's affections, or so he thinks, he boasts 'I have limed her' (3.4.71–2). He refers to the practise of spreading bird-lime, a sticky substance, on branches to catch birds. His use of this image offers us insight into the predatory nature, even the cruelty, of his interest in capturing Olivia. Yet, as we've just seen, Malvolio's ambition and desire for Olivia become the lime that ensnares him, and he becomes the bear to be baited. Indeed, he is routinely described as an animal in the 'box-tree' scene. Maria calls him 'the trout that must be caught with tickling' (2.5.19–20); Fabian says 'contemplation makes a rare turkey-cock of him' (28–9); and then describes him as a 'woodcock' who is approaching the 'gin' or trap (82). While Malvolio might imagine he is ensnaring Olivia, he is the one who falls into a trap and who loses the privileges of human status, coming to be treated as an animal and a source of sport.

We have discussed, in the first scene, the homonym of 'hart' (1.1.16) meaning a stag and 'heart'. This homonym, a favourite in love poetry in the period, with its heavy reliance on the conceit of hunting, recurs elsewhere in the play as well. When Olivia comes upon Sir Toby with his sword drawn against Sebastian, she complains that 'He started one poor heart of mine in thee' (4.1.58). That is, when Sir Toby attacked Sebastian he frightened Olivia who has exchanged hearts with Sebastian and is thus also a hart (or stag) 'started' or startled by a hunter. Olivia says to Cesario:

> If one should be a prey, how much the better
> To fall before the lion than the wolf! (3.1.126–7)

Critics disagree as to who is the lion here and who the wolf. Is Cesario the proud lion and Orsino the ravenous wolf? Or is Olivia lamenting that, if she's going to fall prey, it would have been better to fall to the noble Orsino rather than the heartless Cesario? In either case, Olivia accepts her status as prey. When we trace the imagery of hunting, and the hart/heart homophone in the play, we learn that Olivia and Orsino speak the same language of love, describing it as a hunt, even though they do not wind up together, perhaps because they both use this language to describe themselves as victims or prey. Yet Viola/Cesario and Sebastian do not present themselves as hunters, actively seeking harts/hearts, either. They, too, suggest that love pursues and captures them.

Cut

The play's most infamous example of a word whose meaning has changed over time is 'cut', which has a sexual meaning now lost to many readers. We have already seen that Cesario's name, like Caesar's, may derive from the Latin word for having been cut – in Caesar's case out of his mother's womb, and in Cesario's, perhaps, cut as in castrated. A 'cut' can mean a stroke or blow, as in 'the most unkindest cut of all' in Shakespeare's play *Julius Caesar*; an emotional injury or wound; an 'excision or omission of a part' – and so, by extension, a castrated man and so a dupe or fool or a woman, following the logic by which women are defined by what they don't have, a penis. 'Cut' can also mean the quick transition from one shot to another in cinema; a short cut or shortened route; and the shape of a hairstyle or suit – the latest cut. As a verb, it can mean refusing to acknowledge someone; stabbing; gelding or castrating; slashing prices; skipping class or another obligation; and stepping in front of someone in line. In Shakespeare's time, 'cut' in the phrase 'cut a caper' was a verb that could have a sexual meaning; it could mean dancing, playing a jest or having sex with. When Sir Andrew assures Sir Toby 'Faith, I can cut a caper' and Sir Toby responds 'And I can cut the mutton to't' (1.3.116–17), Andrew's boast about his dancing has a double meaning of sexual prowess. Sir Toby picks up Sir Andrew's word 'caper', and takes it as meaning not a dance move but the pickled bud used as a condiment. He then shifts the meaning of cut to 'carve' and suggests he'll carve mutton to serve with Sir Andrew's caper. But since the word mutton could also refer to a prostitute, Sir Toby also reinforces the sexual meaning of cut. As we have seen, using the same word with a different meaning is called antanaclasis, and this figure is used several times in *Twelfth Night*, suggesting the ways that characters put pressure on one another's words, exploiting the multiple meanings words bear and thus their potential to create confusion.

'Cut' is an astonishingly resonant word, then, and one whose meanings have changed – the cinematic meaning, for instance, is certainly not Shakespearean. But the association of the female genitals with a wound and an absence persists from Shakespeare's time to our own. The slang terms for female genitals such as 'slash' or 'gash' follow the logic of the word 'cut' for female genitals. Before we get to 2.5, Sir Toby gives us a lesson in early modern slang: 'If thou hast her not i'th'end, call me cut' (2.3.181–2). Here he uses 'cut' as a degrading term for lacking male genitals and thus being either a castrated man or a woman and so an object of contempt, a fool. We see a similar slide between disparaging terms for female genitalia and insults today.

Malvolio finds the word 'cut' on the outside of the letter Maria drops in his path. Since few of us now write letters by hand, let us take a moment to think about letters and handwriting, a technology that is becoming obsolete, but was central to the transmission of information and conduct of business and relationships in early modern England. Maria explains her scheme in 2.3. It depends on the idea that Maria's and Olivia's handwriting is interchangeable and on metonymy – that is, the figure by which a body part stands in for the aptitude or achievement associated with it. In this case, the 'hand' stands for handwriting which in turn stands for the writer's intentions. Just as Cesario claims he cannot tell the lady from the servant, Olivia from Maria, when first meeting them both, Maria explains to her co-conspirators that 'I can write very like my lady your niece. On a forgotten matter, we can hardly make distinction of our hands' (2.3.154–6). The forgery that ensnares Malvolio depends on a very common practise at the time, one that might seem remote given how few of us now rely on handwriting. That is, handwriting was both already valued as intimately attached to the writer – so that a document in one's own hand might be valued as an especially intimate or incriminating communication, as evidence of one's own intentions – and recognized as deceptive. Collaboration was part of the culture of letter writing. Monarchs and nobles regularly used secretaries to write their letters; illiterate people, too, hired others to write for them (Daybell; Stewart). A gentlewoman such as Olivia might have dictated a letter to a servant such as Maria. A steward such as Malvolio, a servant with enormous responsibility for managing a household and estate, its personnel, accounts and resources, might have used a secretary himself or served as a kind of secretary with regard to important household correspondence. It was widely known, then, that the person who held the pen was not necessarily the one who stood as a letter's author.

In the sixteenth century, Elizabeth I had Queen Mary Stuart (Mary, Queen of Scots) executed for treason on the evidence, in part, of her letters. Yet, according to a contemporary account of her trial, Queen Mary challenged this evidence, arguing that her letters had been forged. The copies offered in evidence were not in her own handwriting, but rather the copies produced by her two secretaries. Mary warned that 'it might be that these two might insert into her Letters such things as she had not dictated unto them' (Lewis 103) because 'it was an easy matter to counterfeit the Ciphers and Characters of others' (102). Mary insisted 'I am not to be convicted but by mine own Word or Writing' (104). But what constituted her own word or writing, her 'hand'? She and the court did not agree, with fatal consequences for Mary. *Twelfth Night* depends on the confusion between the mistress and the servant's 'hand' but resolves that confusion decisively at the end in order to absolve Olivia of responsibility for the forged letter when Olivia firmly distinguishes her writing from Maria's: 'out of question 'tis Maria's hand' (5.1.341).

Letters were also often delivered by messengers who were given the assignment of supplementing a letter's content – or who might do so without authorization. Note that Sir Toby decides to supplement Sir Andrew's letter. He won't deliver it because it 'being so excellently ignorant, will breed no terror in the youth. He will find it comes from a clodpoll. But, sir, I will deliver this challenge by word of mouth' (3.4.183–6).

What is interesting about this culture of letter-writing in the period is that it troubles the operations of metonymy in much the way the subplot of *Twelfth Night* does. What appears to be Olivia's hand, what Maria presents and Malvolio takes as Olivia's hand, is not her hand. As a negative model of reading, Malvolio tries too hard and misses the boat. He supplies what isn't there and misses some of what is. Malvolio never imagines that someone else might have used Olivia's seal or that the letter might have been forged. He is a credulous reader because he reads what he wants to find in the letter.

But let's return to the word 'cut'. What role does the word 'cut' play in 2.5 of *Twelfth Night*? As we've discussed, many critics refer to 2.5 as the 'box tree scene'. But after learning more about the word 'cut', many students might think of this as the 'cut' scene. Malvolio is already deep in fantasy before Maria hooks him. Note how much Malvolio gives the schemers – and how cleverly Maria has already assessed his character and fantasies so as to work upon them. Before he even picks up the letter, he is already imagining himself as Olivia's consort – and Sir Toby's master. When he evaluates the 'hand' that wrote the letter, based on the superscription (the writing on the outside of the sealed letter), he quickly jumps to the conclusion it is Olivia's. 'These be her very c's, her u's and her t's, and thus makes she her great P's. It is in contempt of question her hand' (2.5.86–8). Sir Andrew asks: 'Her c's, her u's, and her t's. Why that?' (89). Why indeed? Sir Andrew's question prompts the audience. The question arises particularly since neither 'c' nor 'p' appears on the superscription of the letter: 'To the unknown beloved, this, and my good wishes' (2.5.90–1). As has long been observed, Malvolio's words refer here to a common word for the vagina (the cut) and to slang for urination, still in use (peeing). On a stage where there are no actual female bodies, this is a pretty graphic discussion of female genitals (Callaghan, *Shakespeare* 38–9).

Critics have come up with a variety of explanations for Malvolio's remarkable outburst about Olivia's c's, u's, t's and great P's. Leah Scragg argues that this bawdy joke is also warning the audience to beware of pickpockets (5). Spelling along with Malvolio – c-u-t-p – they might think of the cutpurses who frequented crowded theatres and reach to pat their pockets or check for the purses tied to their belts (by strings that the cutpurses would cut). Peter J. Smith counters that it is 'dourly implausible' that a comedy so invested in the unruly would function as 'an early version of a neighborhood watch' (1204). Gail Paster helps us think about the effects of this joke. Perhaps Malvolio imagines that even Olivia's urination is 'great' (compared to other people's). If he reveals here his intimate knowledge of her body, rather than a fantasy about it, this knowledge places him in the position of the servant, the person who empties chamber pots. This entails intimacy but also subordination. Malvolio is, then, as much the butt of this scatological humour as is Olivia (Callaghan, *Shakespeare* 33–4). But, like a humbler Acteon, Malvolio has seen his Diana exposed and lived to tell the tale (Paster, *Body* 30–4; see also Paster, *Humoring* 213–17). Inviting the audience to imagine Olivia urinating, Malvolio levels the difference between himself and Olivia, but also that between Olivia and other women. Whereas Olivia wears a veil when we first meet her and aspires to cloistering herself, shutting her gate to suitors, Malvolio here rips that veil away, revealing her to the audience.

If we see Olivia as a figure for Queen Elizabeth I, then the joking reference to her genitals, and the invitation to imagine them, might have subversive political resonances. Even the queen is or has a cut. Peter J. Smith also argues that when the letter spells out M, O, A, I, letters from Malvolio's name but not in the right order, it places in his mouth a reference to a popular satire on the flushable toilet: Sir John Harrington's *The Metamorphosis of a Jax* (jacks or jakes being a word for a privy). If Malvolio seems to supply the 'cut' and the great Ps, this would be a scatological joke assigned to him by Maria that he doesn't grasp (but if the joke is on him for not recognizing the reference, then generations of critics have been stumped as well).

I wanted to take the time to explore this reference in detail because it both reveals how language changes over time – many readers or spectators will not grasp that Malvolio is referring to Olivia's genitals and even picturing her urinating – and how humour, especially the role of the body in humour, can also stay the same in spite of other changes across time. There are lots of bodily jokes in Shakespeare; they weren't put in just for the 'groundlings' or those who paid the lowest admission price to stand before the stage. Jokes about body parts and bodily functions tend to have wide appeal. But that doesn't mean that they transcend time and class. As we have seen, the passage of time has made these bawdy jokes less accessible. And the effect of this joke on Malvolio can also be to bring Olivia down a peg. In the absence of female actors, it is still possible to place ridicule and even disgust at the female body centre stage.

Suit

Another resonant word with multiple meanings that have shifted over time is 'suit'. Suit can mean a law suit or a suit of clothes, the appeal or suit to a monarch for favour (combining romantic and political aspiration), and a lover's or suitor's suit to or wooing of a beloved. 'The word *suit* was not used to describe romantic courtship until the late sixteenth century; thus, *suitor* originally meant "follower" or one who owed suit, then "petitioner or suppliant" at court, and only later one seeking to satisfy erotic rather than material desires' (Crane 100). The contrast between a legal suit and being a suitor, whether to the court or one's beloved, showcases how the word's shifting meanings hinge on the question of what the suitor seeks. Is the suitor trying to get something through active pursuit or a lawsuit or trying to 'suit' himself to the needs of the other party? A suit of clothes itself has multiple meanings. It could be the suit of livery or uniform servants wore (thus marking servitude), or the mark of being a member of a tradesmen's guild (and thus independent) or the costume an actor wore on stage. The suit Cesario wears as he pursues Orsino's suit is 'unsuitable in as many as three different ways' because it not only conceals Viola's gender but simultaneously conceals and reveals her social status since it is a gentleman's suit identical to Sebastian's and thus not a servant's uniform

(Crane 109). Since the plot hinges on Cesario's ability to adopt a suit identical to Sebastian's and to press Orsino's suit to Olivia by proxy, on Olivia's suit to Cesario, on legal actions or suits against Antonio and the Captain, and, finally, on the fact that the Captain is held at Malvolio's suit and so cannot release Viola's 'maiden's weeds' or female 'suit', the multiple meanings of suit stand at the centre of the play's meanings.

Metal/meddle/mettle

Now let's look at a cluster of homonyms – that is, words that sound the same but have different meanings and, at least today, different spellings. The cluster I'm interested in is metal/ meddle/ mettle. This cluster intensifies in act three, scene four. But Sir Toby first alerts listeners and readers to the sound that connects these homonyms. Just as Sir Toby tunes our ears to hear the word 'cut' as an insult in 2.3 so that we are prepared to guess the answer to Sir Andrew's question 'why that?' in 2.5, so he first introduces a word that will be crucial in 3.4 in 2.5 when he greets Maria in these terms: 'How now, my metal of India?' (2.5.11–12). Here, Sir Toby refers to Maria as a precious metal, such as gold. But the word 'metal' might also evoke the meaning of having a bold spirit, which we'll see below.

The next instance of this word is in its verb form, 'meddle'. 'Meddle' is a verb used to describe the fight Sir Toby stirs up between Sir Andrew and Cesario. Sir Toby admonishes Cesario: 'Therefore on, or strip your sword stark naked for meddle you must, that's certain, or forswear to wear iron about you' (3.4.244–6). The verb 'meddle' means variously: to mix or mingle; to engage in conflict, contend, fight; to combine or blend (related to muddling as in cocktail making); to interfere with; or to have sex with. In that final meaning, 'meddle' is one of many words for sex in early modern culture that suggests that sex is something men do to women. In a variety of sources, for example, 'meddle' is the word used to describe male employers having sex with their female servants (often without their consent). The word 'meddle' alerts us to the connections among what might seem very different actions: mixing with, fighting and having sex with. In its multiple meanings, the word points to the intimate nature of fighting and the violent potential of sex. It reminds us that fighting and sex are both forms of mixing or mingling with one's partner or opponent. Just as Sir Toby urges Cesario to 'meddle' with Sir Andrew, Sir Andrew demurs: 'Pox on't, I'll not meddle with him' (3.4.273). The word 'meddle' from Sir Toby to Cesario and then from Sir Andrew to Sir Toby also reminds us that Sir Toby is cooking up this mingling of the two reluctant fighters. He is forcing them together.

The final homonym in this cluster is 'mettle', a noun. When Fabian offers to make peace between Cesario and Sir Andrew, Cesario leaps at the chance: 'I care not who knows so much of my mettle' (3.4.265–6). 'Mettle' here means, according to the *Oxford English Dictionary*, 'a person's character, disposition, or temperament; the "stuff" of which one is made, regarded as an indication of character'. Critic Mary Floyd-Wilson emphasizes the material nature of this way of thinking about character because of 'its derivation from "metal"—of arms and armor—a derivation that gives it the substantive connotation of the durable "stuff" of which a man is made' (Floyd-Wilson 132). Orsino uses the word with this sense again in the last scene:

> Your master quits you; and for your service done him,
> So much against the mettle of your sex,
> So far beneath your soft and tender breeding,
> And since you called me master for so long,
> Here is my hand: you shall from this time be
> Your master's mistress. (5.1.314–20)

In the first instance, Cesario asserts that he doesn't care who knows what he's made of – that is, that 'I am no fighter'. In the second, Orsino recognizes that Cesario's service has contradicted his mettle. Serving a master required a lower, tougher mettle than Viola's 'soft and tender breeding' and female sex. Sebastian and Antonio both stand in contrast to Cesario and Sir Andrew. When Andrew strikes him, Sebastian quickly rises to the challenge, striking Andrew what appears to be three times ('there's for thee, / And there, and there' [4.1.25–6]). C. L. Barber finds this 'manly reflex' to be 'delightful – almost a relief' after Cesario's reluctance (246).

In all of these exchanges, not only is character – what one is made of – material rather than abstract but it is as much a matter of what one carries outside as what one bears within. To some extent 'masculinity is embodied in the sword' and is thus 'prosthetic', in that it is something anyone can put on or take off (Traub, *Desire* 132; see also Jones and Stallybrass and Fisher). But it is not just a matter of having or wearing a sword, as Cesario and Andrew demonstrate, but of knowing how to wield it. The significance of the sword in proving one's mettle adds a punning twist to the cluster of homonyms we've been considering. For Cesario and Sir Andrew, proving their mettle requires them to meddle with one another using metal swords. According to Gail Paster, 'a man's mettle is signaled by the metal he wears on his person or attempts to purchase' (Paster, *Humoring* 225). If mettle is a matter of metal, then that metal includes not only swords but perhaps also the coins in Antonio's purse. Since mettle is both the substance one is made of and what one has and wears then it's particularly interesting that the 'mettle' of Cesario's sex remains in question to the very end. In Tim Carroll's all-male production of the play at the Globe in 2002, Orsino addressed his 'your master quits you' line to Sebastian rather than Cesario, as if his potential mate's mettle still wasn't obvious to him. The Folio text does not have a stage direction specifying the object of Orsino's address. The bracketed [to Viola] you see in many editions has been added by the editor. The absence of a stage direction in the play leaves open the possibility of ambiguity and mistaken identities, even here at the end of the play.

By drawing attention to homonyms in *Twelfth Night*, I have tried to alert you to the role of sound in linking words and drawing some words and phrases to our attention. To activate the role sound plays in Shakespeare's language, I encourage you to listen to recordings of the plays and to try reading key passages aloud. What does focusing on hearing and speaking Shakespeare's language reveal to us that we might miss if we only read in silence?

Nature's bias

In previous chapters, we've talked about how a speech, exchange or figure of speech can help us unlock a play's meanings. In this chapter, we've seen how much a single word or expression can teach us about Shakespeare's England and the play. I want to conclude this chapter by thinking about how a single line can become a point of contention among critics. This is sometimes called an 'interpretative crux'. The literal meaning of 'crux' is cross – which was once used as a means of execution – but the figurative meaning is something that is so difficult to interpret or explain that it causes pain or torment, 'a thing that puzzles the ingenuity' (*OED*). There are many 'textual cruxes' in Shakespeare, that is, moments in the surviving texts that don't quite make sense and so are puzzles for editors, performers and critics. While it is irresistable to wonder whether Shakespeare meant to plant an enigma or simply made a mistake, we usually cannot determine the cause of these cruxes. Discussion focuses, instead, on their effects. Here I want to talk about a single line that has become the hinge of many influential interpretations of the play. Critics agree it is important but they don't agree on what it means.

The crucial moment occurs at the end of the play. (Note that crucial has the same root as 'crux': That which 'finally decides between two rival hypotheses, proving the one and disproving the other; more loosely, relating to, or adapted to lead to such decision; decisive, critical'. It seems to have been used with this meaning starting in the seventeenth century. In common usage, it means simply 'very important'.) Sebastian turns to Olivia to help her make her peace with finding that she has not married exactly the person she thought she had.

> So comes it, lady, you have been mistook;
> But nature to her bias drew in that.
> You would have been contracted to a maid,
> Nor are you therein, by my life, deceived.
> You are betrothed both to a maid and man. (5.1.255–9)

The line I'm calling an interpretative crux is 'nature to her bias drew in that'. Sebastian refers to a common game called 'bowls' which used heavy or weighted balls (a predecessor to bowling). It was said that a ball drawn to the bias followed an oblique or slanting line, swerving from a straight path to a diagonal one. Those who knew the game and the expression would have recognized Sebastian's turn of phrase. Shakespeare elsewhere refers to running 'against the bias' – that is, following a straight rather than a curving path – as unlucky. But if Sebastian's phrasing would have been familiar, his precise meaning is still uncertain. What is nature's bias? Is Sebastian describing a bias that drew Olivia to Viola, even though she mistook her gender, or that drew Olivia to him? The passage isn't absolutely clear.

For a critic of an earlier generation, the meaning was self-evident. C. L. Barber is again a useful example. Writing in the 1950s, he assumed that nature was heterosexual and that opposites invariably attracted (261). Writing in the 1980s, Stephen Greenblatt agreed but made more of the comparison Sebastian makes between sexual attraction and the game of bowls, by which one must swerve or curve away from the same sex and toward the opposite sex.

> To be matched with someone of one's own sex is to follow an unnaturally straight line; heterosexuality, as the image

of nature drawing to her bias implies, is bent... . Something off-center, then, is implanted in nature – in Olivia's nature, in the nature that more generally governs the plot of the comedy – that deflects men and women from their ostensible desires and toward the pairings for which they are destined. (68)

Thus, for Greenblatt, Sebastian's image explains that 'nature's bias' drew Olivia away from Viola and toward Sebastian. Contrary to modern slang, the 'straight' path was toward the same sex and the 'bent' path was toward the opposite sex. Built into nature, in Greenblatt's reading, is a corrective for an inclination toward the same sex. Greenblatt emphasizes the trajectory of the 'swerve' as the natural bias, from 'the desired object straight in one's path toward a marginal object, a body one scarcely knows' (68).

Several critics have since emphasized this inversion of expectation, the way that, in Shakespeare's era, the 'desired object' was often assumed to be of the same sex. But these critics have countered Greenblatt's assumption of a heterosexual plot, by which nature turns one's gaze ultimately to the opposite sex, emphasizing how the play and other evidence from the early modern period suggest that what is 'natural' is same-sex attraction. In particular, Laurie Shannon argues that in early modern England friendship doctrines idealized the equal and consensual relationship possible between members of the same sex. The rhetoric of friendship was most fully developed with regard to relationships between men. Perhaps *Twelfth Night* dresses Viola as Cesario so that Cesario and Orsino can develop a relationship as male friends. (It should be noted, however, that theirs is also the hierarchical relationship between master and servant, although, like many such relationships, it includes interdependency and intimacy.) Critics used to argue that many of Shakespeare's lovers progressed from same-sex friendship to marriage and that marriage was understood as the more mature relationship. But Shannon's research into early modern attitudes suggests that friendship was often understood as a more intimate and satisfying relationship than marriage, since, unlike friendship, marriage involved the joining of those who are unlike and unequal. As a result people settled for marriage rather than progressed or graduated to it. So while for Greenblatt 'Nature has triumphed' (71) at the end of the play, by causing lovers to swerve from the same to the opposite sex, for Shannon culture has triumphed, leading young people to marriages that go against the bias toward members of their own sex.

It is sometimes argued that fashion or demographics dictate certain changes in interpretation, presumably explaining the difference between Shannon's and Greenblatt's approaches to this textual crux. To claim that fashion dictates trends in interpretation often serves to suggest that nothing important is really at stake for critics. They simply manufacture new readings in order to distinguish themselves from their predecessors. To claim that demographics shape interpretation is to say that as the ranks of literary critics expanded to include a greater variety of people, those people asked different questions and saw things in new ways. Gay critics, it is argued, were able to see the same-sex relationships in the plays that some earlier generations of critics had ignored, disparaged, or downplayed. Female critics found more to say about female characters. Of course, critics' identities do not invariably determine their interests or the kinds of questions they ask. Critics' investments and commitments are varied and unpredictable. I compare these two ways of dismissing new approaches to show that they cancel one another out. If the critic's identity shapes his or her approach, then something far more urgent than fashion is at stake. This is sometimes called politics and disparaged as an axe to grind or as bringing an agenda to the task of literary interpretation (as if it is possible to read without an investment). All critics have responsibilities to the texts they interpret and those texts place certain kinds of limits on them and extend certain invitations to them. Controversy emerges out of the text and is not baggage we bring to or impose on it. What is so fascinating about the debate over the meaning of Sebastian's lines is that all of the critics I've mentioned – of different generations and approaches – focus on the same passage, mobilize considerable research to enable them to understand that passage in its early modern context, and do not agree about what the lines mean.

Critics, then, have disagreed as to whether Sebastian means that 'nature' drew Olivia to Viola or to Sebastian. When was Olivia 'mistook'? When she mistook Cesario for a man? Or when she mistook Sebastian for Cesario? The disagreements don't end there. Critics also disagree about the meaning of Sebastian's last three lines. When he says that Olivia 'would have been contracted to a maid' he clearly suggests that her 'mistake' would have been marrying Cesario/Viola (who might not have agreed to that arrangement). Maid here means a young woman. But Sebastian then reassures Olivia that she was *not* deceived: 'You are betrothed both to a maid and man'. Many critics and editors take Sebastian's final line as a reference to himself as a virgin but surely it could also mean that Olivia chose both maid and man in choosing Cesario (who combines the two in one), and chose both in choosing Viola (a maid) and Sebastian (a man) (Higginbotham; Orgel 56).

Writing matters

Many writers fear that if they focus too sharply they won't have enough to say. But lack of focus is a much more common problem. Papers that assign students to do 'close readings' often yield disappointing results because writers, desperate to find enough to say, cram in every detail they notice, sacrificing organization and argumentation to the quest to include. Yet even as they abandon argument, they often run out of observations as well. This is because they cannot think about details and a big picture at the same time. By starting with details and asking yourself why you notice them you can start to practise a bifocal operation, considering near and far, small and large simultaneously. In this chapter, we have looked at single words, images and lines in order to emphasize how much meaning one can find by looking closely at just a small part of a rich text – and then trying to connect that textual moment to the rest of the play. You always have to be able to explain to someone else why you have chosen the focus you have and why this word, or line, or scene is, for you, a key to understanding the play as a whole. How might the restriction to narrow one's focus to a single word or phrase enable one to achieve solid footing and a clear perspective on the play as a whole? When we focus in, what opens up or out?

Here, I want to propose three exercises designed to help you start preparing to write.

Unsettle your text by editing your own

Another way to prepare yourself to write by zeroing in on parts of the play is to choose a passage and edit it. Select a passage that you find particularly interesting. This can be a substantial speech by one character or an exchange among several. Go to the Internet Shakespeare Editions website (http://internet-shakespeare.uvic.ca/Library/facsimile/). Note that to reach *Twelfth Night* you must first go to First Folio (1623). What differences do you see between the First Folio version of your passage and the edition you are using? You might then also contrast the First Folio to a readily available version such as The Complete Works of Shakespeare (http://shakespeare.mit.edu/). Neither the First Folio nor the MIT online text provides the reader with assistance. Neither version offers notes or glosses. Seeing the text in its naked form can help you think about the kinds of help you need. What words need definitions? What in your passage raises historical questions for you? Returning to the text you are using for your course, look for the kinds of assistance it offers you. What do you think helps you understand the passage better? Are there any notes or glosses that you feel get in your way?

Now prepare your own 'edition' of your passage. If there are differences among the versions, decide which version you will use. In Orsino's first speech, for example, would you go with 'south' or 'sound'? What kinds of punctuation would you choose and why? Are there other changes you would make to render the passage more accessible? We have discussed other valuable resources such as the *OED* and concordances. You might wish to turn to these here as well. These are useful tools. But in preparing to write a paper, don't underestimate the value of **re-reading the whole play**, making notes on your text, using post-its to alert you to important places (and maybe color coding them to help you see patterns of connection), and taking notes. For most topics, you need to collect evidence from across the play. It is always important to think too about context and sequence. Why does this speech occur in this scene? What happens before and after the moment that interests you?

Make a list

When you've narrowed down key passages you want to use in your paper, make a list of all the things you observe about each passage. Don't edit yourself at this point. Don't leave out anything. Just get down everything you notice. Start by marking up the passage, circling or underlining anything that strikes you as important. Then consult this checklist to help you notice even more. Not every question will yield important insights. And you might well want to add additional prompts to your own personal checklist. The point of a checklist like this is to provide you with a toolbox. Many students look at a challenging passage and freeze; they don't know where to begin. This checklist gives you a place to start.

Close reading checklist

- OVERVIEW: What **action, event or experience** is being described?

- Does the passage convey a **sense of place? Of time?**

- If you are interested in a scene, **what has been accomplished by the end of the scene?** What would be missing from the play if you cut it out?

- KEYWORDS: Many literary works have a word or group of words that prove crucial to their meaning. Similarly, characters sometimes have turns of phrase or characteristic expressions that help to set them apart from others. This is sometimes called diction. What words grab your attention? What repetitions do you notice? What words send you looking for the glosses, reaching for a dictionary, or planning to work them into conversation?

- SPEAKER: Who is speaking and how do you know? How does this speech attach to and characterize its speaker?

- SOUND: Read key passages aloud. Are certain sounds repeated? As you read, do you find yourself emphasizing certain words or phrases? If you notice rhyme, which words does it link? What's the effect of sound repeated in a line (**alliteration** – repeating consonants; or **assonance** – repeating vowel sounds; or **homonyms** – two words that sound the same but might be spelled differently and have different meanings)?

- STRUCTURE and SYNTAX:

  Verbs: What are the most important actions in the passage? Are the verbs active or passive? Who is doing what to whom? What tenses are the verbs in?

Pronouns: Are the antecedents clear?

Adjectives and adverbs: At one level, these words are unnecessary. What do they add?

Nouns: What are the most important objects, persons, places or ideas in the passage?

Inversion: Do the sentences in your passage have a simple structure (noun-verb-noun)? If not, how does the more complex structure emphasize some words over others? Where are the most important words placed, for example?

Enjambment: While a single line of verse might be considered to stand alone, a thought often carries over from one line into the next. This is called 'enjambment'. If the passage is set as verse, where do you see a thought carry over from one line to the next and where does a line complete a clause or sentence? What difference does this make? The lineation of prose is more random. It is usually set with justified margins so lines end when the space runs out. But in prose, the punctuation alerts us to the end of units of meaning. That's why teachers try to help you learn how to recognize and avoid comma splices or run on sentences. Those sentences muddy the distinction between one sentence and another and confuse readers.

● **PUNCTUATION:** As we've discussed, punctuation is minimal in the First Folio and will vary from edition to edition. So it is often worth comparing several versions of a given speech or scene to see how they have been punctuated. Punctuation is another clue to what is happening in a passage. We might notice the many questions in Sir Toby's speech to Sir Andrew (in 1.3.120f.) or the dashes. *Twelfth Night* is filled with questions, directed to the self and others. 'The honourable lady of the house, which is she?' (1.5.163). 'Art any more than a steward? Dost thou think because thou art virtuous there shall be no more cakes and ale?' (2.3.112–13). Looking for them can help you identify who asks the most and what kinds of questions characters ask. Dashes often signal a change in direction or interrupting one's self (a rhetorical figure called **aposiopesis**). For instance, when Cesario first presents Orsino's suit to Olivia he interrupts his praise to check that he is addressing the right person: 'Most radiant, exquisite and unmatchable beauty – I pray you, tell me if this be the lady of the house, for I never saw her' (1.5.165–7). When Olivia remembers her first encounter with Cesario, in soliloquy, she reviews his attractions and then stops herself. 'Not too fast, soft, soft—' (1.5.285). The hyphen alerts us to the fact that she has interrupted herself and changed the direction of her thoughts. When Malvolio plans his response to what he thinks is Olivia's letter, he breaks off to remark on how impossible it is to express his certainty that he will get what he wants: '—what can be said?—' (3.4.77–8). You could build a good paper just around questions or interruptions in *Twelfth Night*.

● **RHETORICAL FIGURES:** Does the passage use any rhetorical figures? What is their effect? Return to the list of figures at the end of Chapter 2. Remember that your goal isn't to catalogue figures but to train yourself to notice them, and to develop a vocabulary for talking about figures that matter, figures that offer you a way into what makes the play work.

● **IMAGES:** Sometimes a passage evokes your senses – sight, sound, smell, taste, and touch. Are there any such images in your passage? If so, what is their effect? If there are several images, what is the order in which they are presented and is this sequence significant?

Make a commonplace book

At the end of the previous chapter, I encouraged you to divide the play into parts or roles, breaking a unified whole into pieces. That exercise is a reminder that whatever cohesion a play has was created not just by the author or the script but also by the collaborative efforts of the actors on stage, in the moment. It's also a reminder that, as readers and writers, we take things apart in order to understand them and put them back together in ways that create meaning for us. Early modern readers routinely disassembled the works they read into pieces they could use. One of the ways they did this was through memorizing or writing them down. When Sir Andrew admires Cesario's use of the words 'odours', 'pregnant', and 'vouchsafed', he vows 'I'll get 'em all three all ready' (3.1.88–9). What he means by this is that he will commit them to memory for his own use later. People sometimes did this by writing things down in what was called a 'commonplace book', a personal record of quotations from and comments on reading. Once considered little more than a record of wise or witty sayings, the commonplace book is now recognized as having taken many forms, including scrapbooks of transcriptions, translations, clippings, and wildly various compositions and notes. Commonplace books might include fragments of print pasted onto pages or print pages bound into a manuscript.

You may read the play in electronic form or on paper. But I assume that you annotate it or take notes on it. That's crucial to diving more deeply into it, understanding it better, and beginning to collect evidence for your own analysis. Then it's important to move from the notes on your text to producing your own text. A first step can be creating something like a commonplace book. Go over your notes and cull out the lines and passages you think are most important and make them into a separate document. Once you've isolated the pieces of the text that seem most important to you, you might start to think about how you want to group them or rearrange them. You might also listen to an audio version of the play, see it performed, read it aloud with friends or watch a film version. See which lines and passages leap out for you when you do. Do different parts of the play strike you when you hear it rather than read it?

As a first step in your writing process, try reading and listening as Sir Andrew does, seeking out words, phrases, images and lines that you might yourself want to put to use. Then examine what you've produced. This will probably tell you as much about yourself as about the play, but that's not a bad thing as a start. For many writers, it is most difficult to move from personal appreciation to analysis. In this exercise, start with the assumption that if you wanted to put something in your commonplace book then it is indeed important. You don't need to explain in your paper why it is important to you. Instead, you need to explain why it might be important to someone else. How do the fragments you've collected add up? If you were to take your commonplaces as evidence about the play, what claim about the play might they support? What are your post-its and underlinings telling you about the play?

The next step is to move from commonplacing to **pre-writing**, that is, re-arranging the lines and passages you've collected, grouping some pieces of textual evidence together and thinking about the sequence in which you would like to address the evidence. Might you create several groupings? If so, you either have to explain how they are related or choose one on which to focus. Organizing thoughts and evidence in this way will enable you to combine the research and writing processes and avoid the experience of a blank page or screen. You need not get writer's block yet because you aren't really 'writing' yet. Reviewing your **pre-draft**, you can ask yourself why you made the selections you did and why you have grouped them as you have. Why do these pieces go together? How do they add up? The focus here is developing confidence in your observations as a reader and building on that confidence to grasp that being a writer is being someone who has something to say and the motive for figuring out how best to say it. This process will help you become more self-conscious about paragraphing and the sequencing of paragraphs, transitions, persuasion and building toward a big finish. We'll return to those issues in the final chapter.

The point of these exercises is to help you see that in order to *advance* an interpretation of the play you first need to *retreat*, revisiting the play itself and reflecting on your responses to it. Unsettling the text itself, or taking it apart to form your own commonplace book on it, might seem like moving backwards rather than forwards. But it's the equivalent of Cesario's claim that, if he were to woo Olivia, he would build a willow cabin at her gate. In other words, he would camp out at her door. That's just what you need to do as you prepare to write. You need to camp out at the entrance to the play so that you don't miss anything.

This chapter and the writing exercises I've just described are about slowing down, sharpening your powers of observation, and gathering evidence for your own interpretation of the play. The next question, of course, is how to move from observation to interpretation, from evidence collection to argument? We'll discuss that in the next chapter.

CHAPTER FOUR

From reading to writing

This final chapter focuses on turning enhanced reading skills into writing success. My assumption here is that good writing always begins with **re-reading**. While resources such as a concordance are enormously helpful, nothing can substitute for the process of re-reading a play as the foundation for a good paper. Those who re-read will quickly discover that they have too much rather than too little to say. The next step is winnowing and organizing what you have collected.

I know I can do it. When Maria proposes her scheme to 'gull' or trick Malvolio, making him into 'a common recreation', she concludes 'I know I can do it' (2.3.133). I want you to share Maria's confidence in her ingenuity and her ability to make the most of her wit and writing skill. Maria gets marriage to Toby for her reward. I think you can do better, by making a fulfilling writing process and an excellent paper their own reward. It might also be argued that Maria goes too far, using her writing to bait, madden and enrage Malvolio. We call the sections on writing in this book 'writing matters'. Maria's writing matters in that it has concrete effects in the world, marriage for herself and torment for Malvolio. Maria thus reminds us that writing is powerful. It is not just a dull chore to be crossed off the list, a hoop to jump through. Writing can change lives, secure benefits, impose suffering, entail risk. That's why it's worth doing.

Finding something to write about: questions to consider. A good writer has something to say. All of the exercises in previous chapters have focused on helping you get more out of your reading, collect evidence and begin to build your observations and evidence into an interpretation. We have discussed the importance of questions in *Twelfth Night*. As you re-enter the play in order to prepare to write on it, it helps to organize your thoughts around questions. Framing questions about the play can help to energize your inquiry and your writing. You aren't describing the play. You are trying to ask good questions about it and then working to find answers to those questions. Focusing on questions also helps you think about how to engage other critics, if that is something you are required to do or choose to do. When you highlight questions about the play, you can see that many of these questions are ones that other critics have also asked. You are, then, joining a collective effort to frame good questions about the play and come to some satisfying answers. You can think of critics not as experts who shut down possibilities but as those who share your questions and who may have come to different conclusions than you do. As you'll see in the discussion below, I often use critics to identify good questions about the play rather than as sources of definitive answers about it. So let's think about the play in terms of questions that have inspired critical controversy.

As we have discussed, it can be productive to start at the beginning. **Why does the play begin as it does?** What difference would it make if it began differently – as it often does on stage and screen? It is equally useful to think about the play's conclusion and the process by which it is reached. **How are the plot's dilemmas resolved?** One literary critic suggests that we evaluate a plot and its conclusion by asking this question: Do the characters make their fate or suffer it? (Culler 111). In other words, how actively do the characters work to get what they want? How much leeway does the world of the play offer them to shape their own fates? This is often a productive question to ask about literary works. It's especially interesting with regard to *Twelfth Night* because several of the characters comment on their own agency. When

Viola first proposes to play Cesario she says 'What else may hap to time I will commit' (1.2.57–8). She thus takes matters into her own hands, planning to disguise herself as a man and enter Orsino's service, but also marks the limits of her agency. Only time will tell what will happen when she takes these steps. Responding to her attraction to Cesario, Olivia concludes the first act with this rhyming couplet: 'Fate, show thy force, ourselves we do not owe. / What is decreed must be – and be this so' (1.5.303–4). Since 'owe' here means 'own', Olivia claims that we are not fully self-possessing and almost seems to throw her hands up, surrendering herself to fate. In a soliloquy at the end of 2.2, Cesario comments: 'O time, thou must untangle this, not I. / It is too hard a knot for me t'untie' (2.2.40–1). At this moment half-way through the play, Cesario draws our attention to the play's structure. The complications he has created by disguising his identity – the knot tied by who he is not, by what she has not – constitute the problem the rest of the plot will have to explore and then resolve. This is a double knot: Cesario 'fonds' on his master Orsino but also enjoys being the object of Olivia's desire even as he recognizes that he cannot have both or be both male and female (Traub, *Desire* 131). Finally, Malvolio responds to Olivia's apparent love for him just as Cesario responds to Olivia's overtures and Olivia responds to her own desire: 'Well, Jove, not I, is the doer of this, and he is to be thanked' (3.4.79–80). In this case, however, 'this' is a figment. He is responding not to a real turn of events but to a deceptive 'device', a scheme to trick him. The doer is not 'Jove' but Maria, Sir Toby, and the other pranksters.

Working with these and other passages in the play in which characters comment on their own agency and its limits, make an argument about the relationship between time or fate and individual agency in the play. First, as always, pay close attention to your terms. What are the relationships among fate, time, Jove and individual characters as the agents producing change and resolving problems? Be advised that critics disagree about this. For example, as I've mentioned before, some critics argue that Olivia is humbled for her scorn and withholding in relation to Orsino by falling in love with Viola, an 'impossible object'. By this logic, heterosexual marriage is both what women are supposed to do and a kind of punishment – for women who presume to pick and choose among possible partners. In contrast, other critics argue that Olivia manages to control her own marriage, as few women in the early modern period did. What do you think? Is it fate or agency, discipline or desire that produces the three marriages at the end of the play?

Another way of thinking about the play's resolution is that the main plot is brought to its conclusion by the simple miracle of two. If there is only one Cesario, and he is loved by both Orsino and Olivia, then we have conflict, a conflict that, Orsino makes clear, could turn murderous. If there isn't enough Cesario to go around, Orsino will kill him so that no one can have him. But this is sidestepped by the multiplication of Cesario into Cesario and Sebastian. Orsino is the first to remark on the dazzling doubles: 'One face, one voice, one habit and two persons: / A natural perspective, that is and is not' (5.1.212–13). When he refers to a 'natural perspective' he means an optical illusion produced not by a looking glass or some other sleight of hand but by nature herself – even if, as we now know, identical twins of different sexes are a natural impossibility. (As it turns out, of course, this optical illusion is a matter not just of nature producing identical twins but of Viola costuming herself as her brother. In addition, on the stage, twin-ship itself is a matter of both costuming and wilful suspension of disbelief. Even if twins don't play the roles, and usually they don't, we accept them as identical because we are told that they are and because they are dressed alike.) Bruce Smith suggests that they must sound alike as well or at least that Olivia doesn't remark on a difference (Smith, *Acoustic* 232). Both Olivia and Antonio express wonder at discovering twins – doubled objects of their desire. Antonio's last lines in the play marvel: 'How have you made division of yourself? / An apple cleft in two is not more twin / Than these two creatures. Which is Sebastian?'

(5.1.218–20). Olivia exclaims 'Most wonderful!' (221) and then falls silent for more than 50 lines until she calls for Malvolio, for reasons we'll discuss below. Olivia gets a husband, but it's not clear what happens to Antonio. There are two Sebastians, but neither is for him.

What can we make of what isn't said? What does silence tell us?

The way that Antonio falls silent permanently and Olivia falls silent temporarily in response to the doubling of Sebastian/ Cesario draws our attention to the ways that characters can draw back, leaving us wondering what they are thinking. In the case of Antonio, he not only falls silent but other characters cease to address or mention him. He disappears from the play's attention. But he is standing on stage. What's an actor to do? Viola, too, explains that the Captain holds her maiden's weeds, and that he is in prison 'at Malvolio's suit', and then falls silent for the rest of the play. Here, too, what does the actor playing Viola do? This is a challenge for performance and for interpretation.

Silences have proved to be opportunities for invention. The versions of Shakespeare's plays that were popular in the eighteenth and nineteenth centuries were heavily revised, not only rewriting the language but adding wholly new characters and even changing the endings. Since then, writers have supplied what they think is missing from Shakespeare's plays, doing everything from adding speeches or scenes they feel would enhance a play to writing new versions of the plays with a different emphasis. Often, modern adaptations shift the axis of a play so that a minor character in Shakespeare's version becomes the centre of the new one. Imagine a play that centres on Malvolio, for example, presents events from his perspective, and fleshes out his character. Other writers take inspiration from Shakespeare's stories and then reinvent them for a different time and place. But thinking creatively about what is missing in Shakespeare need not go as far as producing a new work. Every production of a Shakespeare play is a work of interpretation and invention. Since stage directions are so minimal in the First Folio, directors and actors often must decide how a character responds to a revelation (such as the twinning of Cesario and Sebastian). In the many cases in which a character never tells us what he or she thinks or feels, how might an actor add layers of nuance to a performance? Actors sometimes imagine whole histories for a character of whom Shakespeare says little, just to beef up their portrayal. You might think about how you would sketch out a background for a character such as Antonio or Malvolio, or how you imagine the life of Sebastian and Viola before the shipwreck separated them. Think carefully about what evidence the play supplies and how you would attach your speculations to that evidence. What is it in the play that has prompted you to imagine this missing backstory? How do you think your invented backstory sheds light on the play?

As we've discussed, the play's stage directions are often minimal. But sometimes the dialogue itself provides or implies stage directions. This is true, for example, when Sebastian says to Sir Andrew 'there's for thee, / And there, and there', indicating that he hits him three times (4.1.25–6). In 1.5, Sir Toby says 'Tis a gentleman here. A plague o' these pickled herring!' (116–17). In the pause between the two lines, through a long-standing stage tradition, Sir Toby 'makes some kind of noise of indigestion here' (Appelbaum 202). He is, after all, named Belch. This is one of many examples of a silence or gap that becomes an opportunity for directors, actors and critics. On the other hand, critic Robert Appelbaum points out that a habit of filling that silence in one particular way can also prevent us from noticing that it is a silence and that we make a choice to fill it. That is, it isn't inevitable that Sir Toby belches. Many actors playing Sir Toby hiccup at this point, since hiccupping has become a stage convention for drunkenness, although drunken hiccupping doesn't appear to have been an early modern stage convention and hiccupping is not an inevitable response to drinking heavily. Furthermore, what we think a bodily noise means might have changed over time. Historians of the body argue that, in Shakespeare's time, new emphasis was being placed on controlling the body and its emissions, policing the boundaries of the body by means of handkerchiefs, napkins and other ways of cleaning, covering and hiding bodily processes. If Toby belches, hiccups or farts, that tells us a lot about his role in the play, speaking for the irrepressible flesh that can't be disciplined, the pleasures of cakes and ale, eating and drinking. If he makes a rude noise here, is it transgressive – a sign of his defiance of increasingly strict standards for good manners – or simply an amusing reminder of how impossible it is to keep the body under control, even as social custom requires us to do so?

I've alerted you to look for implied stage directions, missing stage directions and silences. We've looked at a few key examples. This is a possible opportunity for your writing, both critical and creative. Where do you see gaps or silences in the play? What do they reveal? And how do you think they might be filled – in performance or in creative writing – using the materials that the play itself makes available? As you may know, those who engage in writing fanfiction or producing fanart inspired by recent media usually accept a certain responsibility to the work that inspires them. Thus every work produced by a fan engages closely with what is often called the 'canon' text. How would you write a proposal for fandrama responding to *Twelfth Night*? To take just one example, fanfiction in the Harry Potter universe is sometimes divided into the following categories (among others): '**Alternative Points of View**' (which in this case might include those of minor, underdeveloped characters); '**I Wonder Ifs**' (possibilities hinted at but not developed in the original); and '**Missing Moments**'. Using these categories, think about *Twelfth Night*. For our purposes here, I would add another category: '**Act Six**'. I've learned this category from students, many of whom think beyond the play's ending. Since the play is named after a holiday, how will the characters be interacting when the next twelfth night comes around? What sequel can you imagine to *Twelfth Night*? As early as act two in the play, Feste reminds us that 'What's to come is still unsure' (2.3.48). At the end, Malvolio's exit and the fact that Viola is still Cesario compound that sense of uncertainty about what is to come.

Here's yet one more category to think with: '**Shadow Stories**'. Stephen Greenblatt refers to 'shadow stories that haunt the plays, rising to view whenever the plot edges toward a potential dilemma or resolution that it in fact eschews' (66). We've already considered how the play threatens Orsino's 'sacrifice' of Cesario. What if he'd gone through with it? The shadow story Greenblatt wonders about in *Twelfth Night* is 'What if Olivia had succeeded in marrying Orsino's page Cesario?' For Michelle Dowd, Viola's story of marrying her master is shadowed by the related stories the play suppresses: of masters who exploit and abuse female servants and then cast them out if they become pregnant; of women driven by economic need, not curiosity or whatever it is that motivates Viola (30). What other shadow stories do you think haunt *Twelfth Night*? What are the effects in the play of gesturing toward these possibilities and then shutting them down?

What are you? Proof and plot

We sometimes describe a good book as a 'page turner'. What that usually means is that it so provokes our desire to find out what happens that we turn the pages quickly and 'can't put it down'. In other media, we now have parallel expressions such as 'binge-watching' a television show that makes us desperate for more and impatient to wait between episodes. There are many reasons to turn pages or binge watch. But one of the things these expressions draw to our attention is the plot and how a plot can make us want to know what happens, to solve a mystery. The connection between plot and the production of knowledge is especially important in the sixteenth century. It has been argued that English drama and forensics grew up together. According to Lorna Hutson, all those who had had 'even elementary lessons in grammar and composition' in the sixteenth century also learned 'ways of thinking about proof and evidence' (1). Playwrights learned how to plot their plays from, among other things, 'the popular practises of detection and evidence evaluation that defined their own culture of trial by jury' (68). Since the jury system became established at the same time that the public theatres flourished, some audience members might also have served on juries. Both activities encouraged them to 'infer past events from insignificant verbal details' (222–3). On the stage, they also saw characters engaged in collecting and assessing evidence, working hard to try to establish that they know what they think they know, but also conceding how inadequate their knowledge is. As an example, *Twelfth Night* is full of misapprehensions. Malvolio, for instance, reads the forged letter just as Maria thinks he will, but in the process he falls into a trap and doesn't understand the letter at all. Antonio mistakes Cesario for Sebastian, as does Olivia. The list goes on.

The fundamental question 'what are you?' appears three times in the play. After Cesario evades some of Olivia's other questions about who he is, where he comes from, and what he wants, she presses him by asking 'What are you? What would you?'(1.5.206–7). Malvolio challenges the rowdiness of Sir Toby and his friends by asking 'are you mad or what are you?' (2.3.85), thus provoking them to turn the accusation of madness onto him. When Antonio intervenes between Cesario and Sir Andrew, taking Cesario's part, Sir Toby says 'You, sir? Why, what are you?' (3.4.310). In each case, 'what are you?' is the way of asking who in the world are you? Cesario, who has evaded other questions put to him, finally answers Sebastian's: 'What countryman? What name? What parentage?' (5.1.227). But those clear answers are not sufficient to wrap the play up. In the play as a whole, who is trying to learn what? What kinds of clues are available to them? What is the relationship between the characters' learning curve and yours as a reader?

What does it take to create an ending?

The idea of plot as a search for knowledge and proof becomes most relevant at the end of the play. As we have discussed, Orsino, Antonio and Olivia all remark on the marvellous resemblance between Cesario and Sebastian. Why, then, do the twins themselves require more proof? Why don't they immediately recognize one another? Sebastian says he would greet Cesario as his sister Viola 'were you a woman', a condition the character Viola supposedly meets. But the play does not draw attention to Cesario's body as the answer to the mystery, although Shakespeare's source does. In the story 'Apolonius and Silla' in Barnabe Riche's *Riche his Farewell to Military Profession* (1581), the Olivia character is pregnant and the complications are only resolved when the Cesario character opens his garments to reveal that he is a she and could not possibly have impregnated Olivia (Wells 182; Gay Intro 5). In Shakespeare's play the gendered body is not the ultimate proof of identity, the bedrock of knowledge. Instead, Cesario shifts from the gender of his body beneath his clothes to his father's body. Cesario announces 'My father had a mole upon his brow' and Sebastian responds 'And so had mine' (5.1.238–9). Each presents a first person singular case rather than merging immediately in the first person plural of twin-ship (our father). Far from opening his garments, this Cesario defers full recognition and reunion until he can change his garments.

> If nothing lets to make us happy both
> But this my masculine usurped attire,
> Do not embrace me till each circumstance
> Of place, time, fortune do cohere and jump
> That I am Viola – which to confirm
> I'll bring you to a captain in this town,
> Where lie my maiden weeds, by whose gentle help
> I was preserved to serve this noble count. (5.1.245–52)

This is one of the most interesting details of the play's concluding scene. Many people miss it because so many productions straighten up the play's ambiguities, dressing Viola as a woman and a bride before bringing the play to a conclusion. Yet, unlike Shakespeare's other transvestite comedy, *As You Like It*, this one defers the appearance of Viola in her 'maiden's weeds' until after the curtain falls. At the very end of the play, Viola is still in the process of becoming herself. Orsino asks to see Viola 'in thy woman's weeds' as a condition not of loving her but of marrying her. When Orsino turns to Cesario it is still as Cesario. As they exit at the end of the play, they do so as Orsino and Cesario. Orsino joins with Cesario in claiming that somehow Viola cannot be recognized as Viola until she has *her* original clothes (and not some other women's clothes). Just as Sebastian greets Viola as his sister only conditionally, in the subjunctive mood ('*were* you a woman'), so Orsino anticipates that when, and only when, they can secure Viola's 'maiden weeds',

> A solemn combination *shall be* made
> Of our dear souls. Meantime, sweet sister,
> We will not part from hence. Cesario, come –
> For so you *shall be* while you are a man;
> But when in other habits you are seen,
> Orsino's mistress and his fancy's queen. (5.1.376–81)

What is the delay? As we have discussed, Malvolio is only recalled at this point in the play because of Viola's desire to reclaim her suit. At the heart of the confusion is a wordplay on 'suit' both in terms of a suit Malvolio has against the Captain and the Captain's possession of Viola's female suit of clothes. The play concludes with the *failure* of Cesario to become Viola and a delay that may be endless. Malvolio is so enraged that it is not clear he can be appeased or that he will release the Captain, enabling him to produce the suit. As one critic puts it, 'we are not optimistic, I think, about the success of this particular pursuit. Malvolio's lawsuit, like the fate of

Antonio, who is also threatened with imprisonment, is left notoriously unresolved by the play' (Crane 112; see also Jones and Stallybrass 199). This conundrum in the play can open up a range of possible topics for a paper. One might be what constitutes proof in the play? Another possible topic is how clothes matter in the play, from Cesario's suit, to Olivia's veil, to Malvolio's stockings, to Viola's maiden weeds.

What does the plot do?

If plots track the unfolding of time, and allow us to collect information and make new knowledge, they also produce various kinds of change. Thinking about what plots accomplish can really help you evaluate a play's meaning. To start with, whom does the plot unite? Whom does the plot divide? (The answers aren't simple. Olivia and Orsino are no longer lovers but they are also rejoined as brother and sister, as are Olivia and Viola). With whom has Orsino fallen in love? With whom has Olivia fallen in love? With whom has Viola fallen in love? Do the characters know the answer? Does it matter? (Note that Orsino has never met Viola and continues to call her Cesario even at the end of the play.)

Critic Stephen Booth observes that 'everything comes together in the last few minutes of *Twelfth Night* and ... nothing does' (185). You might consider using this statement as a jumping-off point for your own analysis of the final scene.

From one perspective, the play ends with three marriages and plans for a big party in Olivia's house. Do you think anyone is excluded from the community assembled at the end? As one example, Sir Toby turns at last on Sir Andrew, whom he's exploited for financial gain: Sir Andrew offers help and Sir Toby says 'Will you help? An ass-head and a coxcomb and a knave, a thin-faced knave, a gull?' (5.1.202–3). On that note, Sir Andrew exits and we don't see him again. As we've just discussed, Malvolio stomps off holding the key to Cesario's ability to reclaim an identity as Viola – and may never surrender that key. What are the consequences of these exclusions? What characterizes the new society created through this comic process? What's missing? Who, if anyone, gets off lightly in your view? Do Orsino and Olivia learn or change in the course of the play? Does anyone? Does Malvolio, for instance, learn anything through the shaming process of ridicule and imprisonment? What choices do productions or films make to emphasize or downplay exclusions? What choices would you make? Finally, consider the possibility that the play doesn't really end in marriage since Orsino and Viola's match is deferred, Olivia's and Sebastian's betrothal has already taken place offstage and we learn about Maria and Toby's marriage, which has also already occurred, by report. Rather than a multiplication of couples, it might be said that the play ends with a lone figure, Feste, and his song is the last word. Consider arguing that marriage is or is not crucial to bringing the play to a close.

What makes for a good marriage in Illyria? Is marriage a happy ending?

Even if we emphasize that *Twelfth Night*, like many comedies, tends toward marriage and seems to use marriage as a mechanism for resolving crisis and imposing closure, the meanings of marriage in the play remain variable and uncertain. Both Orsino and Olivia have opinions about what makes a happy marriage – before they meet their future spouses. Sir Toby says of Olivia: 'She'll not match above her degree, neither in estate, years nor wit – I have heard her swear't' (1.3.105–7). What does this mean? Does it mean that Olivia rejects the idea of subordinating herself to her husband, seeks her equal in estate, years and wit, or seeks an inferior whom she can dominate? When Olivia proposes to Sebastian, she urges him to 'be ruled by me' (4.1.63). When Olivia falls for Cesario, she thinks she's falling for and marrying a servant, but also a gentleman. From the start, she accepts Cesario's insistence that he is a gentleman (1.5.283). In the final scene, Orsino reassures her that, whatever else might be amazing about her match, Sebastian's social status is appropriate: 'right noble is his blood' (5.1.260). (Note that Orsino does not reassure her that 'right appropriate is his gender'.) But what is the appeal of the person with whom she falls in love – a social status equal to her own, a younger or equal age, the same gender, a servant's compliance? We cannot be sure whether Olivia chooses her equal or her subordinate. But we know that, just as Sir Toby predicts, she does not choose someone who is above her. As we have seen, Orsino advises Cesario to marry someone younger (2.4). In doing so, he proposes just the gendered disparity in marriage, with the husband 'above' his wife in years, that, according to Sir Toby, Olivia hopes to avoid. And this is an age disparity that is installed in the relationship between Orsino and Cesario/Viola. What's more, Cesario is prepared to marry the man s/he 'called … master for so long' (5.1.318). When we last see Orsino and Cesario together, they are alike, in that both appear to be men, but at the same time Orsino is 'above' Cesario in years and estate. From one point of view, Viola and Sebastian both marry their masters in that Cesario is a kind of servant to both Olivia and Orsino. Cesario plays on this when he advises Olivia that 'Your servant's servant is your servant' (3.1.100), in other words, that, since Orsino has pledged his service to Olivia, and Cesario works for him, then Cesario is also in service to Olivia. In the final scene, Orsino plays on his history as Cesario's master in order to raise Cesario up to be his equal or even superior: 'Here is my hand; you shall from this time be / Your master's mistress' (5.1.319–20).

In all three of the marriages we see in the play, one spouse pulls the other up in one way or another. Cesario, Maria and Sebastian all marry those of somewhat higher status or at least more established residence than they are. As a reward for her wit, Maria marries her mistress' kinsman. She gets a version of what she's ridiculed Malvolio for wanting. Sir Toby's status in the household is higher than hers. The play downplays financial considerations in these marriages. Sebastian appears to need money, in that Antonio gives him his purse, but Cesario disdains the kinds of tips Feste seems to accept, never mentions need as an incentive for finding a position in an Illyrian household, and so appears not to need money. In choosing Cesario and Sebastian, Orsino and Olivia appear to disregard the issue of a prospective spouse's wealth. Even Sir Toby, who clearly needs money, sets that concern aside in choosing to marry Maria. As he promised from the start: 'I could marry this wench for this device ... And ask no other dowry with her but such another jest' (2.5.176–9). Her wit is her dowry.

In many ways, the early modern stage was preoccupied with cross-class alliances, often between higher-status women and lower-status men. John Webster's play *The Duchess of Malfi*, for example, tells the tragic story of a duchess who marries her steward. In *Twelfth Night*, the aspiration to marry up is derided and punished in the steward Malvolio. While Malvolio attracts his housemates' hostility by being a killjoy, they also use his own social climbing against him. When Malvolio picks up the letter Maria has dropped in his path, he is already fantasizing that he is married to Olivia. For some critics, what happens to Malvolio in the play suggests that crossing class lines is more threatening than cross-dressing, which is easier to reverse and resolve (Callaghan, *Shakespeare* 34). What appears to distinguish Malvolio from characters who achieve marriage is that he is so forthright about the relationship between his ambition and desire. His crime, according to Carol Neely, is desiring Olivia's status and not herself. Neely argues that Malvolio serves as a kind of scapegoat. His tormenters punish him for traits they share. 'Like Malvolio, three of his tormenters are single, impotent men of ambiguous status who seek advancement' (152; see also Malcolmson). His attempt to raise his social status through marriage is punished, seeming to suggest that social climbing through marriage is wrong, even as other characters driven by erotic desire rather than ambition or greed can be allowed to have what they will (Neely 152 passim). In her analysis of Malvolio, Neely insists that the placement of scenes is crucial because those in which Malvolio is tormented for his aspirations comment on and create space for other scenes in which cross-status alliances are transacted.

For our purposes here, what matters is that one can find evidence in the play either to support the argument that the play builds some disparity into every match or that it lines everyone up with someone of the same status. You might argue, on the one hand, that the play eroticizes or romanticizes master-servant relationships, or, on the other hand, that it punishes Malvolio for aspiring to marry his mistress even as it presents master-servant alliances as possible and even romantic. You might argue, in other words, that the play both eroticizes master-servant relationships and punishes Malvolio for his frank desire to secure one. The complexity around this issue is just what would make it a good topic to write on.

And what about love? The word 'love' appears 66 times in *Twelfth Night* and its meanings vary. Characters discuss love for the dead, love they feel and seek, love they cannot feel and cannot reciprocate. They reflect on what love is and should be. They sing and versify about it. Viola personifies love, when she refers to 'the seat / Where love is throned' (2.4.21–2). Olivia accuses Malvolio of being 'sick of self-love' (1.5.86). Critics often form judgements on kinds of love in the play. For example, Viola has been praised for loving Orsino selflessly (Lewalski 175), while Orsino has been criticized as self-absorbed. Can you identify different kinds of love among the characters? What does each contribute to the play and our understanding? In scenes in which you find a concentration of the word love, what do you think the characters are talking about? If two characters are discussing love, as Cesario and Orsino do in 2.4, as we have discussed, do they both mean the same thing by the word? If the play is, in some way, 'about' love, then what does it have to say about love?

Where's Malvolio? Olivia asks this question twice in quick succession, prompting his first entrance after he has picked up Maria's mischievous script for him. 'Where's Malvolio?' she asks. 'He is sad and civil, / And suits well for a servant with my fortunes. / Where is Malvolio?' (3.4.5–7). He then arrives, all dressed up to disappoint her desire for his usual 'sad and civil' or sober and restrained demeanour. You might ask yourself Olivia's question. Where is Malvolio in your understanding of the play? Malvolio is an excellent focus precisely because critics disagree about him and his functions in the play. Audience members often dislike him. But actors love to play his juicy part. And, as I've mentioned before, generations of viewers and readers have understood him as central to the play, as, at some level, the star. Critics cannot agree, however, on whether or not the play depicts him sympathetically. On the one hand, as we have seen, some critics argue that Shakespeare sides with the bears, or, in other words, that the play draws our attention to the injustice of his treatment. Other critics, too, point out that Malvolio is treated more harshly than others who aspire to marry upward, such as Viola and Sebastian, or those whose love makes them foolish (such as Orsino). If it is acceptable for Olivia to marry Sebastian, then why is it laughable for Malvolio to fantasize that she might marry him? Indira Ghose points out that when Cesario and Olivia both draw attention to Malvolio's gentle status at the end of the play, with Cesario describing him as 'A gentleman and a follower of my lady's' (5.1.273) and Olivia as 'poor gentleman' (276) these references to Malvolio as 'one of us', as, like Cesario, both a servant and a gentleman, announce that the joke has gone sour by going on too long. But it's also true that there is a critical tradition of thinking that Malvolio gets exactly what he deserves. Barbara Lewalski, for instance, expresses no sympathy for Malvolio:

> One whose self-regard, self-delusion, and absurd ambition cause him to exclude himself deliberately from human merriment and human love is obviously a greater madman

than the most abandoned reveler or the most fantastic lover in Illyria, and Maria's trick, which causes Malvolio to be taken for a lunatic, points symbolically to the real lunacy of his values. Since he so richly deserves his exposure, and so actively cooperates in bringing it upon himself, there seems little warrant for the critical tears sometimes shed over his harsh treatment and none at all for a semi-tragic dramatic rendering of his plight in the 'dark house'. (Lewalski 171)

What is *your* final assessment of Malvolio and how he is treated?

'A candle and pen, ink, and paper': Getting down to the business of writing

In his confinement, Malvolio depends on writing to convince others that he is not mad and to effect his escape. Like Maria, he finds that writing is a powerful way of expressing one's self, stating one's case and changing one's circumstances. Desperate to communicate with Olivia, he repeatedly asks for the materials needed to write her a letter: 'a candle and pen, ink, and paper' (4.2.81). You may need only a laptop to get writing. Whatever equipment you use, you need to break the writing down into manageable steps.

Fear not foul papers. We have discussed the fact that, for the most part, plays from the sixteenth and seventeenth centuries don't survive in manuscript. What has seemed mysterious, even sinister, to some with regard to Shakespeare is in fact true of all playwrights from the period. We don't have the handwritten rough drafts or final copies of their plays. There are many reasons for this, including the fact that, as we have discussed, the plays were distributed to actors not as complete drafts but divided into individual actors' parts. Although we don't have these drafts, experts in bibliography or the history of the printing of playbooks often speculate about the author's 'foul papers' standing behind printed texts. Foul papers are defined as the author's last complete draft which would later be transcribed, often by a professional scribe, into a more legible 'fair copy'. When editors suspect that a printed play was set from 'foul papers' rather than a 'fair copy' they base this guess on the following character-istics: 1) loose ends, false starts and unresolved confusions in the text; 2) inconsistencies in designating characters in speech headings and in stage directions, particularly exits; (3) unclear and unhelpful stage directions (Donno 165). Thus, although 'foul papers' are a subject of scholarly speculation, rather than surviving evidence, their memorable name conjures up many writers' worst fears about what their drafts look like, even if they are on the screen rather than the page. But every writer needs to go through the draft process. There cannot be a fair copy without first producing foul papers.

The actors from Shakespeare's company who oversaw the printing of the First Folio, which collected most of his plays together, praised Shakespeare for never revising. 'His mind and hand went together: And what he thought he uttered with that easiness, that we have scarce received from him a blot in his papers' (First Folio A3a). This is not an accurate description of Shakespeare's writing practise. The plays themselves provide considerable evidence of revision. For example, in *Twelfth Night*, Viola famously proposes to present herself as a eunuch (or a castrated man) and then never mentions it again (although, depending on how we understand Olivia's attraction to Cesario, mentioning this fiction might have been a useful way to discourage Olivia's interest). Her reference to being a eunuch might refer to a 'eunuch flute', rather than the condition of having been castrated; a eunuch flute was 'a passive instrument through which the voice of another was sounded' (Parker, 'Editing' 56). Viola also claims that she can sing and then never does. Orsino is called both a Duke and a Count. These are signs of a work in progress, a work that Shakespeare changed as he went along. The one piece of handwriting we have that is likely to be Shakespeare's, other than signatures (which notoriously spell his name differently in each case), is a fragment of *The Booke of Sir Thomas Moore* which is 'full of crossed words, rewriting and overwriting' (Stern, *Making* 35). Shakespeare, in short, blotted lines and sometimes should have done so even when he did not. In short, do not aspire to the standard of not blotting. Blot away. Free yourself to write the foul rather than the fair and then do not hesitate to blot out what you don't want to keep.

The **introduction** is one of the most important parts of your paper. In the first few sentences, the introduction engages your reader and helps orient him or her to the text on which you will focus, the topic and your argument. The introduction frames the issue or problem the paper will explore and then articulates the argument that the paper will advance and prove; and it supplies a map of the terrain your paper will cover.

Even though your introduction appears first in the paper, you might consider drafting it last. You should certainly finish the writing process with one final revision of the introduction. This might seem preposterous – which means, literally, working backwards or putting what should come first last. But it makes sense because, in the introduction, you sum up ideas that you have discovered only through re-reading, research, and writing. Students often write their way into an argument, articulating it most clearly only at the end. Take the time to review your paper and revise your introduction to reflect the argument you end up making rather than the one you anticipated making. It's a simple step toward a stronger paper.

Here are some other strategies for writing a good introduction.

1. **Grab your reader's attention – but get to the point.**
   Most writers are so anxious about getting started
   that they begin with general and often meaningless
   sentences. 'Since the beginning of time ...'. As a result,

many papers don't really start until the second or third sentence. It might be true that you just have to write something to get you started. But you don't need to leave it in and your reader doesn't need to read it. Ask yourself exactly when your argument about *Twelfth Night* really gets started and cut out all of the throat clearing and engine revving that precede.

2. **Help your reader out.** Be sure that you identify the author and text you'll be discussing. It is often useful to include a date for your main text as well.

3. **Get specific as quickly as possible.** Sometimes it makes sense to jump right into the text you're discussing. You can use a moment from the play to introduce the topic of the paper and/or the problem your paper investigates:

When Sebastian tells Olivia that she mistook him for Cesario in Shakespeare's *Twelfth Night*, he claims that 'nature in her bias drew in that' (5.1.258). While many critics such as C. L. Barber assume that Sebastian means that nature drew Olivia to a man rather than a woman, Laurie Shannon argues that in the early modern period nature's bias was assumed to be toward likeness. Nature's bias, therefore, would draw Olivia toward Viola rather than Sebastian.

Notice that these opening sentences do not yet articulate the author's argument. Instead, they use other critics to set up a debate or disagreement about what the line means. The author will need to float a new interpretation of this line and position it in relation to what these other critics have said.

This is a good place to observe **the difference between a topic and an argument.** A topic is the subject you want to learn and think more about: clothes in *Twelfth Night* or Malvolio or the meanings of love or madness. Your argument is what you have to say about that topic. Your teacher might propose particular topics to the whole class; as a result, you might share a topic with another student in class. But you need to frame a distinctive and original argument of your own. Most writers will start with a topic and then work their way toward an argument.

4. **Stake a claim or frame a question.** It is useful to think about a claim or thesis as needing to be 'contestable'; that is, your thesis should not be self-evident but rather a claim you will need to support and prove and that you will need to persuade your reader to accept.

5. **Try the formula Context / problem / response.** Sometimes it's useful to use a structure that, by encouraging you to 'fill in the blanks', prompts you to formulate an argument. One such structure comes from the book *The Craft of Research* (Booth, Colomb, and Williams).

   a. Context (contextualizing background): This is the information that helps to orient the reader. Here you establish some common ground that you and your reader can share. What do we need to know to understand what you'll be discussing in your paper?

   b. Statement of the problem.

   c. Your response to the problem.

Here is an example: Context: On Shakespeare's stage, men and boys played all of the female parts. Problem: For many critics this has raised the question of whether the plays reinforce or undermine gender roles. Response: Does it have to be one or the other? I will argue that Shakespeare's *Twelfth Night* both undermines conventional gender roles and reinforces them.

Shaping a strong paragraph. The ease with which we can hit return and create a new paragraph has made it too easy to forget that the paragraph is a crucial building block in your argument. The divisions between paragraphs should not be random or unconscious. They should be purposeful.

In each paragraph, you make a point or ask a question and then assemble the evidence you need to support your point or answer your question. At the end of the paragraph, the readers should feel that we've covered ground and we are moving forward in the argument. The final sentence of the paragraph launches us into the next idea and paragraph.

Think about the paragraph as a **sandwich**. The topic sentence and closing sentence are the bread and the evidence and discussion in the middle form the filling. You have to have all three – a topic sentence, filling and a closing sentence – to have a successful paragraph.

Just as you might save polishing your introduction as one of the last steps in writing a paper so, in **pre-writing**, you can begin with the filling of a paragraph and then build the framework around it. Perhaps there are three or four phrases you've noticed in *Twelfth Night* that you think go together. You can't yet articulate how, but they are linked in your mind. An organizing principle is guiding your selection and grouping of these passages, even if you can't articulate it yet. In pre-writing, type these into your notes. Create space before and after these quotations. Then make yourself fill that space. What is the point you are trying to make? Finally, and perhaps in a writing session on a different day, turn this prewriting into fluid prose, smoothly integrating your textual evidence into your analysis.

A note about sequence. If your paragraphs could be rearranged without revision then you have a problem. One paragraph should build on the last and prepare the way for the next. Your topic and closing sentences should manage the transitions from one point or paragraph to another. The reader should sense an argument developing – building and unfolding from paragraph to paragraph.

A point in support of your argument is not what happens next in the text under discussion. It is, instead, what happens next in your analysis of the text or in your development of your argument. You know you have a problem if your first or topic sentence describes what happens next in the text, rather than articulating what point you want to make next about what happens and why it matters. In discussing a play or another literary text, you might even choose to discuss events out of sequence in the interests of your argument. For example, you might begin with a discussion of the couplings at the end of *Twelfth Night* or you might group together moments from different acts in support of a point about how the characters discuss the relationship between individual agency and fate.

Conclusions. In an early exchange with Sir Andrew Aguecheek, Sir Toby Belch accuses him of coming to 'a false conclusion' and says that he hates a false conclusion as he would 'an unfilled can' – that is, an empty tankard that should be filled with wine or ale (2.3.6). It's useful to think of your conclusion as a container – a can or tankard – because that is a reminder that you have to put something in it. Sir Toby isn't the only one who hates an unfilled can. But don't fill your can-clusion only with repetition. Your conclusion should reiterate your thesis or argument. But it should also reflect on why your argument is important or what's at stake for you in the argument. Think of your conclusion as a space or opportunity for you to take a step back and explore the implications of your argument. Many writers sum this up as entertaining the question 'so what?' Your conclusion is your chance to leave a final impression on the reader. Too often, writers run out of time and run out of steam, limping to a finish at the end. Or the writer only really figures out the argument at the end, but then does not take the time to revise the paper in light of that discovery, building up to a climax and then quitting. Take the time to make the most of your conclusion.

Finally, be sure to provide a **title** for your paper. Titles force you to identify your focus succinctly. For many, the title is an afterthought. But if you slap on a title thoughtlessly – 'Twelfth Night paper' – you miss an opportunity to think about what you are arguing and why you think it is important and to draw your reader's attention to what distinguishes your paper from a pile of others. A vague or generic title suggests that you do not have much to say and that you made little effort. A cluttered title, with too many key words crammed together, will warn a reader that you never really figured out a focus for your paper and included everything you could think of. Titles are the first evidence you give a reader of how much effort you made and what to expect in your paper. Don't ignore this telltale clue yourself. What does your title tell you about your paper? How can you make both your title and your paper stronger?

Twelfth Night has inspired rapturous praise. One critic, for instance, ventures the opinion that it is 'one of the most beautiful man-made things in the world' (Booth 162). It remains one of Shakespeare's most often performed plays, perennially popular. Yet, for that very reason, some theatregoers complain of *Twelfth Night* fatigue. The play also has a central role in the curriculum. It is, for instance, the one Shakespeare comedy currently included in *The Norton Anthology of English Literature*. For many students, as for many playgoers, *Twelfth Night* has the job of representing Shakespeare. Not every student loves the play or even accepts the importance of studying it. For example, on the blog Bad Reviews of Good Books one finds this comment: 'Absolute shit to be perfectly honest' (http://badreviewsofgoodbooks.blogspot.com/2011/01/shakespeare-twelfth-night.html). I don't require you to love the play but I hope you won't dismiss it so completely either. I aim to help you interpret it and I leave it to you whether you appreciate it. In my own experience as a reader, I have special affection for works that taught me to be a better reader in part by inspiring and then rewarding my careful reading and in-depth analysis. My goal is that you might come to regard *Twelfth Night* in this way. Analysis need not defeat appreciation. It can foster it. Shakespeare's plays repay careful attention; they are not impoverished by it. Even if you dislike or resist the play, don't stop there or walk away. Recognize yourself as a critic and your negative views as the beginning of an argument you want to make about the play. As much as you can, try to approach this play and other literary texts as Sebastian approaches shipwreck, crazy love and mistaken identity: ride the wave.

BIBLIOGRAPHY

Adamson, Sylvia. 'Understanding Shakespeare's Grammar: Studies in Small Words', in Sylvia Adamson, Lynette Hunter, Lynne Magnuson, Ann Thompson, and Katie Wales (eds), *Reading Shakespeare's Dramatic Language: A Guide*. London: Arden Shakespeare/ Thomson Learning, 2001, pp. 210–36.

Appelbaum, Robert. *Aguecheek's Beef, Belch's Hiccup, and Other Gastronomic Interjections: Literature, Culture, and Food Among the Early Moderns*. Chicago: University of Chicago Press, 2006.

Barber, C. L. *Shakespeare's Festive Comedy: A Study of Dramatic Form and its Relation to Social Custom*. Princeton: Princeton University Press, 1959.

Belsey, Catherine. 'Disrupting Sexual Difference: Meaning and Gender in the Comedies', in John Drakakis (ed.), *Alternative Shakespeares*. London and New York: Methuen, 1985, pp. 166–90.

—'Shakespeare's Little Boys: Theatrical Apprenticeship and the Construction of Childhood', in Bryan Reynolds and William N. West (eds), *Rematerializing Shakespeare: Authority and Representation on the Early Modern Stage*. Houndmills, Basingstoke: Palgrave MacMillan, 2005, pp. 53–72.

Berry, Ralph. 'Twelfth Night: the experience of the audience', *Shakespeare Survey* 34 (1981), 111–19.

Blake, Norman. *A Grammar of Shakespeare's Language*. Houndmills, Basingstoke: Palgrave MacMillan, 2002.

—*Shakespeare's Language: An Introduction*. Houndmills, Basingstoke: Palgrave MacMillan, 1983.

Booth, Stephen. *Precious Nonsense: The Gettysburg Address, Ben Jonson's Epitaphs on his Children, and 'Twelfth Night'*. Berkeley, CA: University of California Press, 1998.

Booth, Wayne, Gregory G. Colomb and Joseph M. Williams, *The Craft of Research*, 3rd edn. Chicago: University of Chicago Press, 2008.

Booty, John E. (ed.). *Book of Common Prayer 1559: The Elizabethan Prayer Book*. Charlottesville, VA: University of Virginia Press/Folger Shakespeare Library, 1976.

Brathwaite, Richard. *The English Gentlewoman, Drawne out to the Full Body*. London, 1631.

Bullough, Geoffrey. *Narrative and Dramatic Sources of Shakespeare*, Vol. 2. New York: Columbia University Press, 1958.

Callaghan, Dympna. *Shakespeare Without Women: Representing Gender and Race on the Renaissance Stage*. New York: Routledge, 2000.

—*Who Was William Shakespeare?* London: Wiley-Blackwell, 2013.

Carroll, William. 'The virgin not: language and sexuality in Shakespeare', *Shakespeare Survey* 46 (1994), 107–19.

Crane, Mary Thomas. *Shakespeare's Brain: Reading with Cognitive Theory*. Princeton: Princeton University Press, 2001.

Crawford, Julie. 'The Homoerotics of Shakespeare's Elizabethan Comedies', in Richard Dutton and Jean E. Howard (eds), *A Companion to Shakespeare's Works: The Comedies*. Malden, MA: Blackwell, 2003, pp. 137–58.

Crystal, David, and Ben Crystal. *Shakespeare's Words: A Glossary and Language Companion*. New York: Penguin, 2004.

Culler, Jonathan. *Literary Theory: A Very Short Introduction*. 2nd edn. Oxford: Oxford University Press, 2011.

Davis, Lloyd. 'Rhetoric and Comic Personation in Shakespeare's Comedies', in Richard Dutton and Jean E. Howard (eds), *A Companion to Shakespeare's Works: The Comedies*. Malden, MA: Blackwell, 2003, pp. 200–22.

Daybell, James. 'Female Literacy and the Social Conventions of Women's Letter-Writing in England, 1540–1603', in James Daybell (ed.), *Early Modern Women's Letter Writing, 1450–1700*. Houndmills, Basingstoke: Palgrave Macmillan, 2001, pp. 59–76.

Dessen, Alan C. and Leslie Thompson. *A Dictionary of Stage Directions in English Drama, 1580–1642*. Cambridge: Cambridge University Press, 1999.

Donno, Elizabeth Story. 'Textual Analysis', in Elizabeth Story Donno (ed.), *Twelfth Night or What You Will*. New Cambridge Shakespeare. Cambridge: Cambridge University Press, 2003, pp. 163–8.

Dowd, Michelle M. *Women's Work in Early Modern English Literature and Culture*. New York: Palgrave Macmillan, 2009.

Dugan, Holly. 'Scent of a woman: performing the politics of smell in late medieval and early modern England', *Journal of Medieval and Early Modern Studies* 38.2 (2008), 229–52.

Elam, Keir. 'Introduction', in Keir Elam (ed.), *Twelfth Night*. Bloomsbury Arden Shakespeare; 3rd edn. London: Bloomsbury, 2008.

Ferguson, Margaret W. 'Fatal Cleopatras and Golden Apples: Economies of Wordplay in Some Shakespearean "Numbers"', in Jonathan Post (ed.), *The Oxford Handbook of Shakespeare's Poetry*. Oxford: Oxford University Press, 2013, pp. 77–94.

Fisher, Will. *Materializing Gender in Early Modern English Literature and Culture*. Cambridge: Cambridge University Press, 2006.

Floyd-Wilson, Mary. 'English Mettle', in Paster, Gail Kern, Katherine Rowe and Mary Floyd-Wilson (eds), *Reading the Early Modern Passions: Essays in the Cultural History of Emotion*. Philadelphia: University of Pennsylvania Press, 2004, pp. 130–46.

Frye, Northrop. *The Anatomy of Criticism: Four Essays*. Princeton: Princeton University Press, 1957.

Gay, Penny. 'Introduction', in Elizabeth Story Donno (ed.), *Twelfth Night or What You Will*. New Cambridge Shakespeare. Cambridge: Cambridge University Press, 2003, pp. 1–52.

—'*Twelfth Night*: "The Babbling Gossip of the Air"', in Richard Dutton and Jean E. Howard (eds), *A Companion to Shakespeare's Works: The Comedies*. Malden, MA: Blackwell, 2003, pp. 429–46.

Ghose, Indira. *Shakespeare and Laughter: A Cultural History*. Manchester: Manchester University Press, 2011.

Giese, Loreen L. *Courtships, Marriage Customs, and Shakespeare's Comedies*. Houndmills, Basingstoke: Palgrave MacMillan, 2006.

de Grazia, Margreta. 'Homonyms before and after lexical standardization', *Shakespeare Jahrbuch* 127 (1990): 143–56.

Greenblatt, Stephen. *Shakespearean Negotiations*. Berkeley: University of California Press, 1988, pp. 66–93.

Hawkes, Terence. *Shakespeare in the Present*. London: Routledge, 2002.

Higginbotham, Jennifer. 'Fair maids and golden girls: the vocabulary of female youth in early modern English', *Modern Philology* 109.2 (November 2011), 171–96.

Howard, Jean E. *The Stage and Social Struggle in Early Modern England*. London: Routledge, 1994.

Jones, Ann Rosalind and Peter Stallybrass. *Renaissance Clothing and the Materials of Memory*. Cambridge: Cambridge University Press, 2000.

Keller, Stefan Daniel. *The Development of Shakespeare's Rhetoric: A Study of Nine Plays*. Tubingen: Deutsche Nationalbibliothek, 2009.

Kerrigan, John. 'Secrecy and gossip in *Twelfth Night*', *Shakespeare Survey*, 50 (1997), 65–80.

Korda, Natasha. *Labors Lost: Women's Work and the Early Modern English Stage*. Philadelphia: University of Pennsylvania Press, 2011.

Lewalski, Barbara. 'Thematic patterns in *Twelfth Night*', *Shakespeare Studies* 1 (1965), 168–81.

Lewis, Jayne Elizabeth (ed.). *The Trial of Mary Queen of Scots: A Brief History with Documents*. Boston: Bedford/ St. Martin's Press, 1999, pp. 93–120.

Malcolmson, Cristina. ' "What you will": Social Mobility and Gender in *Twelfth Night*', in Valerie Wayne (ed.), *The Matter of Difference: Materialist Feminist Criticism of Shakespeare*. Ithaca, NY: Cornell University Press, 1991, pp. 29–57.

Mallin, Eric S. *Inscribing the Time: Shakespeare and the End of Elizabethan England*. Berkeley: University of California Press, 1995.

Manningham, John. *The Diary of John Manningham of the Middle Temple ... Barrister-At-Law, 1602–1603*. John Bruce (ed.). Westminster: J. B. Nichols for the Camden Society, 1838.

Marcus, Leah. *Puzzling Shakespeare: Local Reading and Its Discontents*. Berkeley: University of California Press, 1988.

McDonald, Russ. *Shakespeare and the Arts of Language*. Oxford: Oxford University Press, 2001.

McMillin, Scott. 'The Sharer and His Boy: Rehearsing Shakespeare's Women', in Peter Holland and Stephen Orgel (eds), *From Script to Stage in Early Modern England*. Houndmills, Basingstoke: Palgrave Macmillan, 2004, pp. 231–45.

Mentz, Steve. *At the Bottom of Shakespeare's Ocean*. London: Continuum, 2009.

Moglen, Helene. 'Disguise and development: the self and society in *Twelfth Night*', *Literature and Psychology* 23 (1973), 13–20.

Montrose, Louis. 'The Elizabethan Subject and the Spenserian Text', in Patricia Parker and David Quint (eds), *Literary Theory / Renaissance Texts*. Baltimore: Johns Hopkins University Press, 1986, pp. 303–40.

Murfin, Ross and Supryia M. Ray (eds). *The Bedford Glossary of Critical and Literary Terms*. Boston: Bedford/ St. Martin's Press, 1998.

Neely, Carol. *Distracted Subjects: Madness and Gender in Shakespeare and Early Modern Culture*. Ithaca: Cornell University Press, 2004.

Orgel, Stephen. *Impersonations: The Performance of Gender in Shakespeare's England*. Cambridge: Cambridge University Press, 1996.

Osborne, Laurie E. *The Trick of Singularity: Twelfth Night and the Performance Editions*. Iowa: University of Iowa Press, 1996.

—' "The marriage of true minds": Amity, Twinning, and Comic Closure in *Twelfth Night*', in James Schiffer (ed.), *Twelfth Night: New Critical Essays*. London: Routledge, 2011, pp. 99–113.

Palfrey, Simon and Tiffany Stern. *Shakespeare in Parts*. Oxford: Oxford University Press, 2007.

Palmer, D. J. '*Twelfth Night* and the Myth of Echo and Narcissus', *Shakespeare Survey* 32 (1979), 73–8.

Parker, Patricia. 'Editing Puzzles and Eunuchs of All Kinds' in James Schiffer (ed.), *Twelfth Night: New Critical Essays*. London: Routledge, 2011, pp. 45–64.

—*Literary Fat Ladies: Rhetoric, Gender, Property*. London: Methuen, 1987.

—*Shakespeare from the Margins: Language, Culture, Context*. Chicago: University of Chicago Press, 1996.

Paster, Gail Kern. *The Body Embarrassed: Drama and the Disciplines of Shame in Early Modern England*. Ithaca, NY: Cornell University Press, 1993.

—*Humoring the Body: Emotions and the Shakespearean Stage*. Chicago: University of Chicago Press, 2004.

Pennington, Michael. *Twelfth Night: A User's Guide*. New York: Limelight, 2000.

Pentland, Elizabeth. 'Beyond the "lyric" in Illyricum: Some Early Modern Backgrounds to *Twelfth Night*', in James Schiffer (ed.), *Twelfth Night: New Critical Essays*. London: Routledge, 2011, pp. 149–66.

Potter, Lois (general editor). *Revels History of Drama in English*. IV: 1613–1660. London: Methuen, 1981.

Powers, Alan W. ' "What he wills": Early Modern Rings and Vows in *Twelfth Night*', in James Schiffer (ed.), *Twelfth Night: New Critical Essays*. London: Routledge, 2011, pp. 217–28.

Puttenham, George. *The Arte of English Poesie* [1589]. Edward Arber (ed.). London, Alex. Murray, 1869.

Ravelhofer, Barbara. "Beasts of Recreacion": Henslowe's White Bears', *English Literary Renaissance* 32 (2002), 287–323.

Read, Sophie. 'Puns: Serious Wordplay', in Sylvia Adamson, Gavin Alexander and Katrin Ettenhuber (eds), *Renaissance Figures of Speech*. Cambridge: Cambridge University Press, 2007, pp. 81–94.

Scragg, Leah. 'Her C's, her U's, and her T's: why that?' a new reply for Sir Andrew Aguecheek', *Review of English Studies* N. S. 42.165 (1991), 1–16.

Sedinger, Tracy. ' "If Sight and Shape Be True": the epistemology of cross-dressing on the London stage', *Shakespeare Quarterly*, 48 (1997), 63–79.

Semenza, Gregory M. Colón. *Sport, Politics, and Literature in the English Renaissance*. Delaware: University of Delaware Press, 2004.

Shannon, Laurie. 'Nature's bias: Renaissance homonormativity and Elizabethan comic likeness', *Modern Philology* 98 (2000), 183–210.

Smith, Bruce R. *The Acoustic World in Early Modern England: Attending to the O-Factor*. Chicago: University of Chicago Press, 1999.

—' "His fancy's queen": Sensing Sexual Strangeness in *Twelfth Night*', in James Schiffer (ed.), *Twelfth Night: New Critical Essays*. London: Routledge, 2011, pp. 65–80.

Smith, P. J. '*MOAI* "What should that alphabetical position portend?" an answer to the metamorphic Malvolio', *Renaissance Quarterly* 51 (1998), 1199–224.

Spurgeon, Caroline. *Shakespeare's Imagery and What It Tells Us*. Cambridge: Cambridge University Press, 1935.

Stern, Tiffany. *Documents of Performance in Early Modern England*. Cambridge: Cambridge University Press, 2009.

—*Making Shakespeare: From Stage to Page*. London and New York: Routledge, 2004.

Stewart, Alan. *Shakespeare's Letters*. Oxford: Oxford University Press, 2008.

Traub, Valerie. *Desire & Anxiety: Circulations of Sexuality in Shakespearean Drama*. London: Routledge, 1992, pp. 117–44.

—*The Renaissance of Lesbianism in Early Modern England*. Cambridge: Cambridge University Press, 2002.

Tudor, Elizabeth. 'Armada Speech to the Troops at Tilbury', in Leah S. Marcus, Janel Mueller and Mary Beth Rose (eds), *Elizabeth I: Collected Works*. Chicago: University of Chicago Press, 2000, pp. 325–6.

Vickers, Nancy J. 'Diana Described: Scattered Woman and Scattered Rhyme', in Elizabeth Abel (ed.), *Writing and Sexual Difference*. Chicago: University of Chicago Press, 1982, pp. 95–109.

Wales, Katie. 'An A-Z of Rhetorical Terms', in Sylvia Adamson, Lynette Hunter, Lynne Magnusson, Ann Thompson, and Katie Wales (eds), *Reading Shakespeare's Dramatic Language: A Guide*. London: Thomson, 2001, pp. 271–301.

Wells, Stanley. *Shakespeare: A Life in Drama*. New York: W. W. Norton, 1997.

Wilson, Richard. *Secret Shakespeare: Studies in Theatre, Religion, and Resistance*. Manchester: Manchester University Press, 2004.

Further reading, viewing, and browsing

Numerous resources are available to help you understand Shakespeare better and write about his works more effectively. Many students want to know more about Shakespeare himself. A good place to start is Dympna Callaghan's *Who Was William Shakespeare?*, which combines biography with an introduction to all of his works. Samuel Schoenbaum's *William Shakespeare: A Documentary Life* (Oxford: Oxford University Press, 1975) remains a classic. It compiles the evidence that every biographer relies upon to tell Shakespeare's story. It thus demonstrates that we do, in fact, have information about Shakespeare. He is not the mystery that popular conspiracy theories sometimes claim. Schoenbaum's volume also allows you to assess some of the key pieces of evidence for yourself. To understand early modern theatre and Shakespeare's place in it, you might turn to another sourcebook, Tanya Pollard's *Shakespeare's Theatre: A Sourcebook* (Malden, MA: Blackwell, 2004).

There are many companions and guides to Shakespeare study. I recommend *A Companion to Shakespeare*, David Scott Kastan (ed.) (Blackwell, 1999); *A Feminist Companion to Shakespeare*, Dympna Callaghan (ed.) (Blackwell, 2000); and *A Companion to Shakespeare's Works: The Comedies*, Richard Dutton and Jean E. Howard (eds) (Blackwell, 2003).

Websites

The map of early modern London online (http://mapoflondon.uvic. ca/index.htm).
   This site includes a digital atlas and an encyclopedia of early modern people and places.

The Official Website of the British Monarchy (http://www.royal. gov.uk/ HistoryoftheMonarchy/KingsandQueensofEngland/ KingsandQueensofEngland.aspx).
   This website offers you a quick and authoritative overview of who was included in the Tudor or Stuart dynasties as well as basic information on a given monarch, such as Elizabeth I.

Internet Shakespeare Editions website (http://internetshakespeare. uvic.ca/Library/facsimile/).
   This site provides versions of all of the plays and poems in quarto (where a quarto exists) and First Folio versions. This is a great resource for easy access to the Folio version of *Twelfth Night*. The site also includes a database of performance, containing information on over 2,300 productions on stage and film, as well as substantial resources on Shakespeare's life and times.

The Complete Works of Shakespeare (http://shakespeare.mit.edu/).
Digital, public domain editions of all of Shakespeare's works but not searchable.

Online Shakespeare Concordance (http://www.opensourceshakespeare.org/concordance/).
This is an easily searchable concordance. To find a word or phrase in a particular play, use the advanced search function in the concordance. For an overview of where a word appears in all of Shakspeare's works, use the keyword search page (http://www.opensourceshakespeare.org/search/search-keyword.php). This will show you how many times the word appears in Shakespeare's works and where.

Shakespeare Line Count (https://sites.google.com/a/shakespearelinecount.com/www/shakespeare-characters-line-count).
This website gives you line counts for the major characters in each play, but not the minor ones. One might dispute some of the totals but this tool gives you a quick overview of who has the most lines in a given play.

Shakespeare's Words (http://www.shakespeareswords.com/).
This is an online version of David Crystal and Ben Crystal's book *Shakespeare's Words*: *A Glossary and Language Companion* (Penguin, 2004). The site not only allows you to search for a word or phrase in all of Shakespeare's works, as the concordance does, but also to search in a glossary of the word's early modern meanings. Searching 'cloistress', for example, will show you that its only appearance is in *Twelfth Night* and that it means 'cloistered nun, member of an enclosed order'. Access the search function here: http://www.shakespeareswords.com/Search.aspx. Whereas the *Oxford English Dictionary* is a subscription service and so can only be accessed from networked computers that subscribe, this is a freely accessible database and so an invaluable resource.

Shakespearean Promptbooks of the Seventeenth Century (http://bsuva.org/bsuva/promptbook/)
Promptbooks document a particular production of a play, including marginal notes on props, blocking and movement. The promptbooks in this collection are from seventeenth-century productions.

Shakespeare Resource Center (http://www.bardweb.net)
This website collects links to many internet resources on Shakespeare.

Shakespeare's Globe (http://www.shakespearesglobe.com/education/library-research/library-archive/recommended-online-resources)
The Globe is a reconstruction of Shakespeare's theatre and a focus of research on Shakespeare, his theatre and the history of performance. This is their list of recommended online resources.

Touchstone (http://www.touchstone.bham.ac.uk/)
This site focuses on resources for Shakespeare study in the United Kingdom. Its most interesting feature is an 'enquiry service', which allows you to submit questions and receive help on where to find the resources you need.

Mr. William Shakespeare and the Internet (http://shakespeare.palomar.edu/)
Provides an annotated guide to scholarly and popular resources on Shakespeare available on the internet as well as its own original contributions, such as a Shakespeare timeline. A treasure trove of information.

Writing resources

Purdue Online Writing Lab (http://owl.english.purdue.edu/owl/)
This website offers resources on the writing process, on mechanics including grammar and punctuation, and on research and citation. It also includes exercises, which can provide invaluable practise.

University of Chicago Writing Program list of grammar, style and usage guides (http://writing-program.uchicago.edu/)

Yale College Writing Center Advice for Students (http://writing.yalecollege.yale.edu/advice-students)

Useful editions

Shakespeare, William. *Twelfth Night: Or What You Will*. Keir Elam (ed.). The Arden Shakespeare. Third Series. London: Bloomsbury, 2008. All citations of *Twelfth Night* in this volume refer to this edition.

Twelfth Night: Texts and Contexts. Bruce R. Smith (ed.). Boston: Bedford, 2001. This volume offers both an edition of the play and editions of a wide range of early modern texts, most presented in brief excerpts, on topics including the literary genre of romance, music, sexuality, clothing and disguise, households, puritanism, and clowning and laughter. There is a substantial introduction as well as helpful introductions to these topics and to the individual texts.

New Cambridge Shakespeare Twelfth Night. Elizabeth Story Donno (ed.). With an Introduction by Penny Gay. New Cambridge Shakespeare. Cambridge University Press, 2003.

Cambridge School Shakespeare: Twelfth Night. Rex Gibson (ed.). Cambridge: Cambridge University Press, 2005.

The Norton Shakespeare. Stephen Greenblatt, Walter Cohen, Jean E. Howard and Katharine Eisaman Maus (eds). New York: W. W. Norton, 1997. Quotations from Shakespeare plays other than *Twelfth Night* in this volume refer to this edition.

Films

Twelfth Night. Or What You Will. Directed by Tim Supple. 2003. Made for British television by Projector Productions.

Twelfth Night or What You Will. Directed by Trevor Nunn. 1996. Renaissance Films.